# JEWISH BIALYSTOK

## AND SURROUNDINGS IN EASTERN POLAND

# BIAŁYSTOK REGION
## (VOIVODSHIP)

POLAND

DĄBROWA BIAŁOSTOCKA

SUCHOWOLA

KUŹNICA

GDAŃSK   OLSZTYN

SZCZECIN   BIAŁYSTO

POZNAŃ   WARSAW

WROCŁAW   ŁÓDŹ

KATOWICE   LUBLIN

KRAKÓW

(19)   JANÓW

KORYCIN

JASIONÓWKA

SOKÓŁKA

(18)

KNYSZYN

KRYNKI

TYKOCIN   WASILKÓW   SUPRAŚL

(18)
CHOROSZCZ   (66)   GRÓDEK

BIAŁYSTOK   MICHALOWO

ŁAPY   ZABŁUDÓW

SURAŻ   NAREW

NAREWKA

BIELSK PODLASKI

BRAŃSK   HAJNÓWKA

(19)   ORLA

BOCKI

KLESZCZELE

MILEJCZYCE

SIEMIATYCZE

DROHICZYN   GRABARKA

MIELNIK

N

0   10   20   30   40   50                    100 km

*Map by Eric Nyhus*

*Tomasz Wisniewski*

# JEWISH BIALYSTOK
## AND SURROUNDINGS IN EASTERN POLAND

*A Guide for Yesterday and Today*

Translated from the Polish by
LUCYNA ALEKSANDROWICZ-PEDICH

Edited by
DAVID AND ELLEN ELLIOTT AND JILL SIMONSEN

*With a foreword by Mimi Sheraton*

THE IPSWICH PRESS
*Ipswich, Massachusetts 01938*

# ACKNOWLEDGEMENTS AND NOTE TO READERS

The Publisher is grateful to the archives, institutes and individuals indicated in the photograph captions for the use of their photographs in this book. (The initials "TW" refer to the author, Tomasz Wisniewski, and "DHE" refers to one of the editors, David Elliott.)

Special thanks are due to Mimi Sheraton for the Foreword and to Samuel Gruber for the useful Glossary (Appendix IX).

The small-format town maps are the work of Iwona Wisniewska-Plichta. Eric Nyhus designed the maps for the frontispiece and for Appendix X.

Readers should be aware that, for technical reasons, Polish names and terms appear in the text in Anglicized form instead of with the more exact orthography achievable with the use of Slavic linguistic software.

Readers' comments, corrections and suggested additions for future editions would be welcome.  Please send them to:

- The Ipswich Press, Box 291, Ipswich, MA 01938, or
- Tomasz Wisniewski, Box 351, 15-001 Bialystok, Poland

Published by
THE IPSWICH PRESS
Box 291
Ipswich, Massachusetts 01938

# CONTENTS

*Author's Dedication*

This book is dedicated

*tobie*

that is, to you into whose hands it has found
its way, in the hope that you will find it helpful.

With special thanks to Ellen and David Elliott, American Peace
Corps volunteers, for their faith, friendship and support.

T.W.

"You are going *where*?"

That was the standard reaction of friends when I first announced I would be traveling to Bialystok in the fall of 1992. "But *why*?" was the next most frequently asked question. Why, indeed, would one choose to go to this virtually unknown city in the northeast corner of Poland? Other than those who go on business, most of the visitors are Holocaust survivors or their descendants who make the sad pilgrimage to visit the nearby memorial of the Treblinka concentration camp, or the site of Bialystok's Great Synagogue, which was burned with 800 Jews inside by the Nazis on June 27, 1941. Since both sides of my family came from other areas of Poland, I had no associations with this city, other than a mild interest in the place that was home to Ludwik Zamenhof, the creator of the international language, Esperanto, and of Stalin's infamous and crafty foreign secretary, Maxim Litvinov. Hardly reasons for a visit to so remote an area.

My answer probably provoked even more incredulity. I wanted to visit Bialystok to taste *bialys* on their home ground, just as I had gone to Scotland for the celebrated salmon, to Denmark for its legendary pastry, and to Istanbul for the sweet chewy candy that is called Turkish delight.

For those unfortunates who do not know the savory *bialy*, let me say that it is an irregularly round, squashy roll—homely and homey, a yeasty onion and poppy-seed-flecked treat most often served in the United States for breakfast as an alternative to the bagel. More formally known as *Bialystocker Kuchen* (*Kuchen* from the German word for cake although the unsweeted *bialy* is definitely bread), it was presumably created in that city by Jewish bakers and identified with it at least as far back as 1835, according to my findings.

Undoubtedly a variation on the larger, round and level *pletzl*, this smaller version, with its identifying center well, was so popular that inhabitants of that city were known elsewhere as

*"Bialystoker kuchen fressers"—fressers* meaning lusty and prodigious eaters.

Having loved *bialys* as far back as I can remember, and knowing I would be in Poland on an assignment, I decided to pursue this gastronomic research, and so, on a cold and rainy day in October, my husband and I, with a car and driver made the three-hour trip from Warsaw to Bialystok. A part of Russia until 1918, Bialystok had been home to over 70,000 Jews, of whom only five were said to remain at the time of our visit. Thus did I make the sad finding that no one now in Bialystok had ever heard of these magical *kuchen.*

That I met anyone at all, and had a trip so interesting that I began work on a book about this historic bread and the lives and destinies of the people who cherished it three times a day, was due to the knowledge and generous cooperation of Tomasz Wisniewski. This thorough and interested historian dug up facts, photos and assorted remnants of the bread's history and ultimately lead me to many rewarding contacts with *Bialystocker Landsleit* (émigré organizations) throughout the world, most especially in the United States and Israel. Subsequently I also came in contact with branches in Paris, Melbourne and Buenos Aires.

What emerged was a picture of a particularly stalwart and feisty group of people—inventive, industrious and productive, and with an inordinate pride in having come from Bialystok, even though they all are haunted by the bitter memories of their tragic departures. Time and again my thirty or so respondents from all parts of the world wanted to be sure I knew that their home city had been a thriving center of wood, leather, iron and textile production, as well as of theater and literature, and that about 80 percent of the population had been Jews. And, as I was reminded by Israel's former prime minister, Yitzak Shamir, who spent two years in Bialystok's prestigious Gymnasium, that city was an early and fervid center of the Zionist movement.

Its more illustrious sons include Dr. Albert Sabin, who developed the polio vaccine that bears his name, and Samuel Pisar, the highly-respected international lawyer and author of *Of Blood and Hope*, a memoir of his childhood in Bialystok and internments at Auschwitz and other equally infamous camps. Dr. Ivan Selin, the former chairman of the United States Nuclear Regulatory Commission, and his wife, Nina (the descendant of three generations of bakers in Bialystok who made the famed rolls) also visit-

ed that city and benefited from Tomasz Wisniewski's charm,
knowledge and his willingness to share it.

I now have the names of over a dozen *bialy* bakers and their
former addresses, and I intend to return to Bialystok for a memorial walk through all of these landmarks so that I can bring the
epic story full circle.

Suffice it to say that I will rely on the cooperation and guid-
ance of Tomasz Wisniewski, who surely knows everything there is
to know about Bialystok, past and present, trivial and crucial, sad
and joyous. I would advise any other visitor to do the same, and
this fine and detailed book makes his experience and knowledge
available to all.

*Mimi Sheraton*
*New York, 1998*

## PROLOGUE

If the Jewish history of Bialystok and the surrounding region is to be preserved, it must be renewed through visits by its Jewish descendants so that it can continue to exist in the national memory of the Jewish people. To this end, this guidebook sets out to assist former inhabitants of the area, their children and grandchildren, as well as others who wish to visit the region or simply learn more about it.

In these pages, we also hope to correct the widespread misconception that the only Judaic landmarks in the region are those found at the synagogue in Tykocin. In fact, Bialystok, Krynki, Knyszyn, Drohiczyn, Bocki, and Jasionowka are all well worth visits despite the fact that information about them is hard to come by. Polish guidebooks published abroad seldom mention them, probably because the historical information has just not been known or easily accessible. And, of course, neither Judaic historical research nor tourism were encouraged during the Communist era.

For instance, very few people know that before World War II, many groups (and not just Jewish ones) visited the town of Zabludow (20 km south of Bialystok) to view its famous 17th-century wooden synagogue. However, few of those visitors continued on to Bialystok. Today, the situation has been reversed, and it is now visitors to Tykocin who often return directly to Warsaw without stopping to see Zabludow. By traveling just 30 minutes longer, these visitors could reach Bialystok, which serves as an excellent base for at least two or three days' exploration of the city and surrounding area (including Zabludow).

This guidebook, however, aims to be more than just a modern-day Baedeker. It strives also to lead readers back into the past by means of historical information and photographs. Through these materials, those who are unwilling to leave home or to experience first hand the heartbreak of the annihilated past will be able to visit this important region.

In Bialystok a common wall separates the untended Jewish cemetery from its Catholic counterpart. In the dark hours of late afternoon and evening on November 1—the date Poles traditionally celebrate the memorial Day of the Dead holiday—the two necropolises stand side by side in silence, one lit with thousands of candles commemorating those who have departed this world, the other barely visible through a curtain of darkness. In recent years, though, a relatively new phenomenon has been observed: On each successive November 1, more and more candles illuminate the silent, once-forgotten Jewish cemetery as the residents of Bialystok come to pay their respects. Though not truly their own, the necropolis strikes a chord in the collective memory of the citizens of Bialystok. And in so doing, it becomes theirs as well.

Although the Jewish cemeteries in Bialystok have been closed to new burials for many years, some of Bialystok's older Jewish residents decided to remain in Poland after the war, wishing to be buried in the land of their ancestors. As Feliks Malarewicz, one of Bialystok's last Jews, used to say, "A place for me should be found somewhere here."

Let this guidebook, then, serve as another candle in the common consciousness of the Jewish and Polish people—one whose flame of memory will strengthen with each passing year.

## AN INTRODUCTION TO THE BIALYSTOK REGION

Bialystok is a city, the largest in northeastern Poland, with a population of 280,000. Bialystok is also the name of a *voivodship*, which is akin to a "county" or "province." This *voivodship*, one of 49 such in Poland, encompasses the region that this book describes. It has a population of about 700,000 and an area of 10,000 square kilometers (about 125 km north to south and 80 km east to west). (See map facing title page.)

Lightly populated, it is a land of open space, farmlands, evergreen forests, clean air, and light industry. The major farm crops are oats, rye, wheat and, especially, potatoes. Most of the agricultural acreage, however, is grassland, feed for the dairy cattle that make the region Poland's first in milk production.

The Bialystok region's unspoiled, natural environment is highlighted in the south by Bialowieza National Forest, today Europe's largest primeval forest (145,000 acres), and in the north by Biebrza Landscape Park, Europe's most extensive natural marshland. The region's lush, green river valleys and untouched forests are home to many unusual bird species, which each year attract a growing number of birdwatchers from around the world.

*Early photographs of towns in Bialystok region near Belarussian border: (above)* **Nowy Dwor,** *marketplace in 1923; markings indicate two synagogues no longer standing (photo courtesy Moshe Verbin.) (below)* **Hajnowka,** *pre-World War II, synagogue with columns in rear*

On the east the region borders Belarus (formerly called Byelorussia). Since the 11th century the region has changed hands several times between Poland, Lithuania and Russia. During the years of Poland's "partition" (1795 to 1918), the region was part of Russia. Today the area is ethnically diverse, with primarily Polish people, but also Belarussians, Russians, Ukrainians and even a few Tartars and Jews. While 95 percent or more of the people in Poland are Roman Catholic, it is estimated that in the Bialystok region more than 25 percent are Russian Orthodox.

The Bialystok region is rural, quiet, with a peaceful, unspoiled veneer. Beneath the surface is its rich Jewish history .

## Jewish Settlement in the Bialystok Region

Polish-Jewish relations date back to the 10th century, when the first Jewish communities appeared in this part of Europe. In 1264, Prince Boleslaw, the Pious of Kalisz, issued a body of laws known as the Calisian Statute which guaranteed Jews the right to live in

*Bialystok: Jewish fish market in 1927; no longer in existence (photographer unknown; collection TW)*

the towns of western Poland. This right was extended to Jews throughout Poland in 1334 by King Kazimierz Wielki (Casimir the Great). However, Jewish settlements did not spring up in the Bialystok region of northeastern Poland (historically known as the Podlasie region) until after those in neighboring Mazowsze and Lithuanian lands. In fact, it was not until the 16th century that any true Jewish settlements existed in the region—in towns such as Tykocin, Drohiczyn, Bielsk Podlaski, and Suraz and in villages such as Orla and Jasionowka. Although Podlasie's first Jewish inhabitants actually appeared in the 14th and 15th centuries (in Bielsk, Drohiczyn, and Mielnik), their numbers were so few they could not be considered communities until much later.

Tykocin is home to the region's oldest Jewish community, formed in 1522 from a settlement founded by the Jewish community of Grodno (now a city in Belarus and 70 km northeast of Bialystok),which itself dates back to 1389. From its nucleus of nine families, Tykocin's Jewish community grew in power until by the

mid-18th century it had become the most important community
(or *kahal*) in Podlasie to command the Jews of Podlasie. Tykocin is
also the site of the region's first Jewish cemetery (1522).
Excavations in the late 20th century in the center of the town of
Bielsk Podlaski uncovered human remains that may well have
come from another equally old Jewish cemetery, one abandoned
in the 16th century when Jews were expelled from that town after
a conflict with Christians.

Over the next few centuries—most notably the 19th and early
20th—Jews settled in Podlasie in increasing numbers. By 1897, the
Jewish population of the Bialystok region (which encompassed
approximately the same area as the present Bialystok *voivodship)*
accounted for 58.3 percent of the region's urban inhabitants, making it truly "the heart of European Jewry." According to Antoni
Sujkowski *(The Geography of Old Poland,* Warsaw, 1921), the
Grodno province, which included large parts of the Bialystok
region, was then home to 350,000 Jews, comprising 17.4 percent of
the population, the highest in any Polish province. In other
provinces the breakdown was as follows: 13 percent of the population in Vilno province, 12 percent in Vitebsk, 16 percent in
Minsk, 12 percent in Mohylev, 13 percent in Volhyn, 12 percent in
Podole, and 12 percent in Kiev. For the entire kingdom of Poland
the figure was 13 percent. By 1939, Jews inhabited 40 of the towns
and villages in the Bialystok region.

## AN ANALYSIS OF LOSS

Despite the region's large Jewish population prior to World War
II, little remains to remind us of their presence in Bialystok and
the surrounding area: a few old synagogues (which were rebuilt
after the war and today are museums, cinemas, galleries, sport
halls, and warehouses), some Jewish cemeteries (albeit neglected
and overgrown), and scattered Jewish ritual bath houses (*mykvas*),
hospitals, schools, and shelters for the poor.

### Cemeteries

Before World War II, the present Bialystok region was home to 37
Jewish communities, only five of which did not have their own
cemeteries (Bialowieza, Lapy, Hajnowka, Suprasl, and
Starosielce). Altogether, the area contained as many as 47 grave-

yards, both functioning and closed. To give you an idea of their distribution, Bialystok had four (originally six), Wasilkow three, and Bocki, Dabrowa, Choroszcz, Jasionowka, Jalowka, Orla, and Zabludow two each.

Although the word *cemetery* can scarcely be applied to a place with only a single surviving *mazeva* (tombstone) or a plowed field surrounded by a wall, in many cases that *is* all that remains of these burial grounds—a piece of land, a fragment of a wall, a lone *mazeva*. If we count these, as many as 30 Jewish cemeteries remain in the region. If, however, we acknowledge only those with at least half their burial stones intact, the number of Jewish cemeteries in the area is very few indeed—Krynki and Knyszyn are but two examples.

Fifteen years ago in Bialystok's central park (between Kalinowskiego and Mlynowa streets) I found a *mazeva* from a cemetery established there in 1752. In the 1970s a single burial stone could be seen in each of two cemeteries in Bocki (currently, only one remains). In Jalowka you will find one *mazeva*, in Grodek several, in Suraz nine, and in Wasilkow thirteen.

*Bialystok: Jewish cemetery on Wschodnia Street. (above) gate; (below left) plaque on gate; (right) gravestones in winter (photos TW, 1989, 1994)*

In the largest Jewish cemetery in northern Poland—the 13-hectare (32-acre) burial ground near Wschodnia Street in Bialystok—approximately 7,000 burial stones remain. Data from the city hall archives indicates that between 1890, when the cemetery was founded, and 1943, 500 graves were added each year. According to our calculations, this means that by 1941 the cemetery had 34,500 *mazevas*. For names that could be deciphered on remaining *mazevas*, see Appendix IV.

According to our best estimates, approximately 14,000 of the 180,000 to 270,000 *mazevas* that could be found in Bialystok-area cemeteries in 1939 remain today, plus at least 1,000 in Krynki, Sokolka, and elsewhere whose weight caused them to sink beneath ground level. The first *mazevas* to disappear were those that were of either artistic or material value, molded out of marble, sandstone, or granite. Ironically, in some cases vandals helped to preserve *mazevas:* In the cemeteries in Narewka and Mielnik, for example, "treasure hunters" turned collapsed *mazevas* face down, thus preserving their original colors.

Today, Jewish burial grounds can be found under plowed fields and forests (Niemirow), behind gated walls (Siemiatycze), in the foundations of postwar homes (Siemiatycze), and beneath the cobbled roads near Grodek and the asphalt roads leading to Orla and Narewka. In Jasionowka, burial stones were used to build part of the street in front of the school. In Ciechanowiec (in the Lomza region), Germans used them to construct a dog pound; in Krynki a warehouse. In the stairways leading to houses (for example, near the cemetery in Bialystok), schools (Siemiatycze), and even in Christian cemeteries (Suprasl) *mazevas* lurk. Unaware of the profanity, local people even used sandstone *mazevas* to fashion knife sharpeners and axes.

## Synagogues

The loss of Jewish architecture is easier to assess because many of the destroyed structures were considered masterpieces and had been documented and described prior to World War I. By the end of World War II, however, not a single wooden synagogue remained: those that were not destroyed initially were later used as warehouses, only to be burned or blown up by the retreating Germans. In addition, many of the 18th- and 19th-century brick synagogues were destroyed as well—most notably those in Krynki, Jasionowka, and Knyszyn. Only a few were saved.

Bialystok is in some ways typical of the entire region: Of the 59 synagogues and houses of prayer that were in use in 1939, only four remain. In Warsaw, a city 15 times larger than Bialystok, approximately the same number survived. According to our calculations, in the area covered by this book between 160 and 165 synagogues existed prior to World War II, 80 of which were constructed of brick. The following stand today: four in Bialystok; three in Krynki (one in ruins); one each in Mielnik, Milejczyce, and Orla; and one synagogue and the Talmudic house in Siemiatycze and in Tykocin. Others—such as the synagogues in Suchowola, Bialowieza, and Sokolka—have been rebuilt and bear little resemblance to the original structures. And at least two of the most magnificent brick synagogues—those in Tykocin and Orla—were spared destruction.

As we begin our exploration of the Bialystok region, one fact becomes startlingly clear: Despite the almost total annihilation of the Jewish people and their material culture—synagogues, cemeteries, and cultural artifacts—much still remains to remind us of their presence. To give you an idea of the cultural significance of this region, let's take a look at some of the highlights:

• **The Jewish cemetery in Bialystok.** The largest Jewish necropolis in northern Poland, this cemetery contains a pillar commemorating the 1906 ( June 1 to 3) pogrom provoked by the Russian Army (see photo). One hundred ten Jews were murdered. (See details on page 56)

• **The Jewish cemetery in Tykocin** (35 km west of Bialystok). Predating even the Jewish cemeteries in Lublin and Cracow, this cemetery was started in 1522 and is one of the oldest preserved cemeteries in Poland. (See details on pages 30-31.)

• **The Jewish cemetery in the typical** *shtetl* **of Krynki** (55 km southeast of Bialystok). With more than 3,000 mazevas, this burial ground is the largest remaining Jewish *shtetl* cemetery. Excluding the city of Lodz itself, the 3,000 *mazevas* found here are more than

*Bialystok: monument to victims of 1906 pogrom (photo TW, 1989)*

you will find in the Pila, Poznan, Suwalki, Lomza, and Lodz regions combined. (See details on page 85.)

- **The Jewish necropolis in Knyszyn** (27 km north of Bialystok). Situated on the remains of 16th-century dams and royal ponds, this cemetery is built on one of the most unusual sites in Europe. (See details on page 81.)

- **The "rebuilt" cemetery in the small town of Bransk** (50 km south of Bialystok). Between 1987 and 1993, volunteers recovered, moved, numbered, and fenced in nearly a hundred *mazevas* (mostly 19th century) that they had collected from area sidewalks, roads, and curbs. (See details on page 68.)

- **The ghetto cemetery in Bialystok.** These unique remains—on Zabia Street in Bialystok—represent the only remnants of a ghetto cemetery in Europe. Opened in 1941, it was used as a cemetery until 1971.

- **Jewish forest cemeteries.** Rarely encountered elsewhere in Poland, these sites are likely to surprise mushroom hunters and other explorers in the Bialystok region. Miraculously, at one of these cemeteries—in Narewka—the colors of the *mazevas* remained intact, including one stone covered with real gold.

- **The synagogues of Tykocin and Orla** (30 km west and 63 km south of Bialystok, respectively). These two synagogues are special. Both are unusually large 17th-century synagogues and both retain many of their original architectural details. They are two of the oldest surviving synagogues in Poland and the two oldest in northern Poland. Tykocin dates from 1642; Orla probably from the late 1600s.

- **The unique 18th-century *mykva* (ritual bath) in Bocki** (68 km south of Bialystok). Considered a rarity on the national scale. Of the few *mykvas* surviving in Poland, the one in Bocki is probably the oldest.

- Old *shtetl Hasidim* synagogue in Krynki (55 km southeast of Bialystok). One of the very few Hasidim synagogues which remain in Poland.

- Talmud school buildings in Tykocin and Siemiatycze (30 km west and 114 km south of Bialystok, respectively).

There is more to remind the visitor of the former Jewish presence in the Bialystok region than these synagogues, graveyards, and official buildings. As you wander through the area, you will

*Tykocin: local Jewish theatre company (photo TW, 1994)*

detect many signs of the Jewish rural colonies that flourished here between 1850 and 1937: the stamp of the excellent Sholem Aleichem Jewish Library on a book from an antiquarian bookstore; a detail from the Star of David on a wall, a wood board in an old building, or a door frame; the empty space a *mezuzah* once occupied. All of these things remind us of a culture and community that once thrived here and must now not be forgotten.

And in small ways the region's Jewish legacy *does* live on among its current Christian inhabitants. Jewish words have become ingrained in the Polish language, Jewish foods such as *maza* bread are popular, in kitchens some dishes such as carp are prepared in the traditional Jewish way. In the towns in the region one finds streets honoring Jews: in Bialystok, Icchok "Malmed," a ghetto hero, and Ludwik "Zamenhof," inventor of the Esperanto language. Some businesses still bear Jewish names; and there are plaques on numerous buildings in Bialystok and other large towns identifying the former site of a synagogue, or Jewish school or hospital. In the museums there are Jewish paintings and other memorabilia.

## Beyond the Jewish Tradition

The culturally diverse Bialystok region has much to recommend it besides its Jewish past: 18th-century wooden mosques, the Muslim cemeteries of Kruszyniany and Bohoniki, wooden windmills dating from the 18th century, wooden Eastern Orthodox chapels—all of which bear witness to the coexistence of a melange of cultures and nationalities over many centuries. Today many such examples of wooden architecture can be found in the open-air museums (*Sconsins*) on the outskirts of Bialystok and in Bialowieza.

Take a photograph of the Branicki Palace in Bialystok. Inhale the fresh air and encounter a bison in Bialowieza, the oldest natural forest in Europe. Poke through the remains of the Russian czars' hunting lodge at Bialowieza. Visit Grabarka (near Siemiatycze), one of the most important Eastern Orthodox pilgrimage sites in the world (and home to the only orthodox nunnery in Poland), and wander through the forest of pilgrims' crosses that surround the church (the water from the nearby spring is believed to be imbued with miraculous qualities). Go canoeing on the Narew, Biebrza, or Suprasl rivers, or fishing on beautiful Lake Siemianovka.

There is beauty to experience here in every season: In summer and fall, mushrooms of incredible quantity and quality carpet the region's woods; in winter cross-country ski trails beckon, and sightseers can explore the area on skis or sleds, or glide down the ski slope in Ogrodniki (near Suprasl); in spring, tens of thousands of birds arrive from all over the world.

If you're convinced now, then off we go!

## Getting There

The city of Bialystok can be reached by train, bus, car, bicycle, or foot. You can even charter a private airplane or helicopter if you so desire! (There is a small airport on the city's outskirts used mostly by small private planes.) For those without a car, the train is probably the best option. It will get you from Warsaw to Bialystok in about three hours, proceeding along an increasingly attractive rural route, over several rivers and through forests and marshlands.

If you travel from Warsaw to Bialystok by car, you may chose to stop about halfway at Treblinka, site of the infamous death camp. Between 1942 and 1943 more than 800,000 Jews perished here. The camp site has been turned into a moving memorial in the form of a symbolic graveyard. There are thousands of symbolic tombstones, each representing a town whose Jews were killed in the camp. All the Jewish towns in the Bialystok region are represented.

*Treblinka: (above) stone slabs representing railway tracks leading into death camp; (below) stones representing towns from which Jewish victims came (photos DHE, 1993)*

Traveling by car, you might wish to make Tykocin your next stop. We suggest you spend an hour or two in Tykocin before proceeding to Bialystok and your hotel. (See the Appendix VII for specific tourist information.) If you are traveling by train, you can take the overhead footbridge across the tracks of the Bialystok railroad station to reach the bus depot, where buses depart every half hour for Tykocin.

## TYKOCIN

*Population 2,055*

*35 km west of Bialystok and 150 km northeast of Warsaw.*

Tykocin needs little introduction. So vital is its role in the history of the Jewish people that a visit to Tykocin—in *Polin* (Hebrew for Poland)—has become an essential part of the educational curriculum of thousands of young Jews from all over the world. In 1994 alone more than 30,000 tourists visited its Judaic Museum, and in 1992 the town served for the third time as the destination of the famous March of the Living, a special education program for young Jews from all over the world.

### History

Established in 1424 on the picturesque left bank of the Narew River, Tykocin is the oldest town in Podlasie. Once rich and full of life, the town today is quiet and a bit sleepy, as if missing some vital element. In the middle of the 16th century, King Sigismundus Augustus built a fortified castle in Tykocin, which served as one of the most powerful lowland strongholds in Poland. The castle functioned as the King's private residence, and in addition to the royal arsenal it contained a library and treasury. A royal mint was located in town, and a river harbor near the castle was used to send grain to Gdansk.

Jews first settled in Tykocin in 1522, under a "privilege" granted by King Augustus to buy land, build houses, own any kind of business, build a synagogue, and open a cemetery. This privilege was confirmed and expanded by subsequent privileges in 1536, 1576, and 1639.

In the years after its establishment, the Jewish community in
Tykocin flourished. Fortuitously located on a waterway at the
crossing of major trade routes joining the lands of the Great
Duchy of Lithuania with Mazovia and even Western Europe,
Tykocin was one of Podlasie's most significant towns. And
Tykocin's merchants—some of them Christians but most of them
Jews—journeyed to the markets of Hamburg, Vienna, Leipzig,
and Nuremberg. With a population double what it is today,
Tykocin's wealth and prosperity endured through the end of the
18th century. In both 1765 and 1893, for example, the Jewish population exceeded the total population of the town today. And in
1765 (just before a partition of Poland), the 2,694 Jewish inhabitants in Tykocin and the surrounding villages comprised the fifth
largest regional *kahal* in Poland—after Brody, Lwow, Leszno, and
Kazimierz (near Cracow). At varying times, the Tykocin *kahal's*
sphere of influence ranged from 100 to 150 km in all directions.
The Jewish community in Bialystok—established at the end of the

18th century—for
many years was
under the authority
of the Tykocin *kahal*,
to whom they paid
their taxes. The 1772
census of the Polish
Kingdom named
the Tykocin *kahal* as
the first Jewish com-
munity "after
Cracow." Like many
other Polish towns,
Tykocin's impor-
tance dwindled
after the "final parti-

*Tykocin: Great Synagogue (1642), now in use as
museum and occasionally as Jewish house of prayer
(photo TW, 1995)*

tion" of Poland between Russia, Austria, and Prussia in 1795.
     There is considerable historical evidence that Jews traditional-
ly supported Poles against foreign domination. During what the
Polish people refer to as "the November Uprising" of 1830-31, the
Jews of Tykocin supported this Polish rebellion against the
Russian empire. General Ignacy Kruszewski wrote in his memoir,
"Several tens of Jews walked forward from Tykocin with a wel-

come; they were happy, and were urging us to take the town, assuring us that the Moskale [Russians] had already escaped." Even as the town itself declined, Tykocin's Jewish population continued to grow. In 1799, 1,653 Jews were 57 percent of the population. In 1862, the 3,545 Jews were 73 percent of the town's population. From this peak, however, the Jewish population began a decline that continued through the end of the century. At the outbreak of World War II, about 1,800 Jews comprised 44 percent of the population of this town of Jews and Catholics.

Tykocin's dual-religion heritage is still clearly visible today in its geographical boundaries. The Motlawa Stream flowing into the Narew River divides the town into its Christian section on the east and its former Jewish section on the west; the two principal houses of worship stand on opposite sides of the market area. Beyond each—again in opposite ends of the town—are the Jewish and Christian cemeteries.

A footnote to the history of Tykocin: The famous poet and scholar Rebeka (Rivka) Tyktiner was born in Tykocin in the early 16th century. She was the first recognized Jewish woman author in Poland. Following in the footsteps of her scholarly father, the local rabbi Mejer Tyktiner—who himself published several religious books in Cracow in 1588—the talented Rebeka wrote *Meneketh Ribhka* in Yiddish. This book, published posthumously in Prague in 1609 and in Cracow in 1618, expounded upon the duties, rights, and obligations of Jewish women. The views she expressed—for example, that lay subjects should be taught in schools—were courageous and progressive for the time.

## The Great Synagogue

As you head toward the town's Western quarter—Kaczorowo—you will encounter the Great Synagogue. Profaned during the last war, the temple has since been rebuilt, with renovations completed in 1977, and now functions as a museum although services are still held here at the request of visiting Jews.

Built in 1642 (about 120 years after the initial Jewish settlement) to replace its wooden predecessor, the synagogue in Tykocin remains one of the oldest and best preserved sites of orthodox Jewry in Poland. Modeled after a 1640 fortified synagogue in Pinsk, Belarus, rather than after the temples of Ukraine, it was built on a square plan. The structure originally supported a typical Renaissance roof with an attic like those found in the synagogues of Husiatyn, Zolkiew, and Szarogrod. However, after a town fire in 1730, the Tykocin synagogue was restored with a high mansard roof. As you approach the temple, its large red roof complete with a signature (avebell) comes into view before the fortified synagogue itself. Opposite the synagogue, Jewish brick houses dating from the 18th and early 19th centuries enclose the synagogue courtyard. Unfortunately, the market stalls—which were built in 1735 and surrounded the synagogue—have not survived. There were 22 stalls of which 16 were attached to the temple itself. When the synagogue was renovated in the 1970s, however, the stall foundations were preserved, and the museum administration hopes to have them rebuilt in the future.

The synagogue incorporates low annexes which surround it on three sides. They formed an entrance hall and separate quarters for women and now house frequently changing exhibits, including a large scale model of the town as it looked before 1939. In the 18th century a tower with a turret was added on the northwest corner, which combined with the altered roof gives the synagogue an appearance more baroque than Renaissance in design. The most striking feature of the rabbi's house, which stood beside the synagogue until its destruction during World War II, was its high, steep roof, which can be seen in the model of the town inside the museum.

Before entering the synagogue, try to evoke the image of the Jewish Orthodox quarters. In *Oppidum Judeorum* (the Jewish city) there were two marketplaces: the Jewish market (today it's the "Old Market," on the banks of Motlawa stream) and the horse market (today the site of a gas station). In addition, a small market operated in front of the synagogue. Surrounded by its stalls as if in a ring of defense, the Great Synagogue dominated the neighborhood of predominantly wooden houses.

*Tykocin: interior of Great Synagogue (photo Szymon Zajczyk, 1930; courtesy of Institute of Art PAN, Warsaw)*

## Inside

If you are lucky, you will meet museum director Ewa Wroczynska upon entering the synagogue. Having been with the museum for years, she knows just about everything there is to know about the temple—and she even speaks Hebrew! However, don't despair if you are not lucky enough to encounter Ewa. The other museum staff members are also knowledgeable and will be able to answer any questions you may have.

To reach the main prayer hall, you must descend a few steps. Restricted by Christian church regulations, synagogue builders were under no circumstances to allow synagogues to tower over churches. However, these architects wished nonetheless to create the sensation of height to reflect the words of the psalmist: "From the heights I call you, Lord!"

Mounted on the wall next to the door between the entrance hall (*pulish,* or meeting place, of the *kahal*) and the main prayer room is a *mezuza* donated by former Bialystok residents Chana and Szamaj Kiselsztejn, who now reside in Israel. Their gifts also include a beautifully embroidered pillow, a Seder tablecloth made by Chana, and a plate for the *Pesach* (Passover) holiday.

Based on a structure of nine parts, the temple's layout is easily discernible. The ninth middle section is taken up by a two-story *bimah* (pulpit) whose four powerful columns support the ceiling. The elevated *bimah* includes a place for the *mohel's* leather armchair, from which he observes circumcisions.

*Aron Ha Kodesz* (the ark) is in the eastern portion of the synagogue. The ark's polychrome sculpted decoration makes it appear similar to those found in Christian churches. The words "This is the Crown of Torah" are inscribed on the upper portion of the decoration, and the sides are adorned with pictures of liturgical vessels—a bowl and a jug. Renovations uncovered polychromy with remains of gilding dating from the 17th century.

The synagogue's walls are decorated with colorful plant and animal motifs as well as with tables containing Hebrew and Aramaic inscriptions dating from the 17th through 19th centuries. The oldest of these inscriptions (1642) is located above the arch of the *bimah* on the northern side. Dr. Aleksandr Pakentreger, Polish historian and specialist in Hebrew, reconstructed and provided contemporary translations for these inscriptions in the late 1960s.

Prior to World War II, the Tykocin synagogue was home to a magnificent collection of synagogical objects, most of which were stolen by Bolsheviks or Germans during that war. For example, Father Kazimierz Cyganek, a parish priest in Knyszyn in the 1930s, wrote of the Tykocin rabbi showing him a painted treasure chest which, according to legend, was carried by Spain's Rabbi Wulf to Tykocin after the Jews were expelled from that country in the 15th century.

Display cases in the synagogues's main hall contain the objects of worship and items of daily life that survived the Holocaust, only a few of which belonged to this synagogue before 1939. Of particular interest is the *Torah* and its decorations, hooks and crowns, menorahs, candlesticks, ritual and domestic vessels, balm containers, *Chanukah* lamps, *Seder* plates, *Kidush* cups, and glasses for *Pesach*. Few museums in Poland have such a beautiful collection. One of the cases also displays a complete set of prayer cloths. To the right of *Aron Ha Kodesz* is a *parochet* (ark cover) donated by the New York Jewish community in 1981.

With so little to remind us of the synagogue's former glory, it is left to the visitor to imagine how it must have appeared before the Holocaust. Picture it, then, illuminated not by electricity but by the hazy light cast by low suspended candles of fantastic shapes merged with the natural light admitted by high windows, and you begin to capture the mood of elevated awe that incited religious exultation in the synagogue. Contrast this with the lower parts of the synagogue that remained in darkness, and you begin to get an idea of the unusual, almost otherworldly atmosphere that permeated this place of worship. This would have been so especially during the night services introduced by Izaac Lurie, "The Holy Ari" who died in 1572.

In addition to the magnificent *Aron Ha Kodesz* and *bimah*, numerous other liturgical objects and skillfully sculpted benches filled the synagogue in its pre-Holocaust days. Embroideries covered the doors of the ark closet containing the Torah scrolls, and the *bimah* tables were covered in grand fashion. On one such table lay a small pillow which the rabbi would sometimes strike with a board to seek silence from the noisy faithful. The rabbi would also hold a silver object in his hand that resembled a narrow bar complete with a finger-shaped cast. This he used to follow the lines of the Torah.

Everywhere there would have been glasses, cans for fragrances, candlesticks, decorated cases, chandeliers, menorahs, containers for hand washing, collection boxes, and religious books. In the corner, or in the entrance hall, there would have stood a velvet or satin canopy resting on four sculpted pillars that was used for wedding ceremonies. From behind the barred windows of the women's quarters would have come the murmurs of quiet prayers.

Before leaving the synagogue, follow the entrance hall to the narrow curving staircase leading to the tower. In its two rooms (one on each floor), you will find a re-creation of the Seder feast and a rabbi's room.

*Tykocin: wooden house near synagogue with Star of David window (inset) (photos TW, 1989)*

Arranged to resemble a typical living room, the room in which the Seder feast takes place contains a table with Seder bowl, decorated cutlery, silver cups, china plates, and a crystal decanter. There is also a copy of a picturesque colorful Hagada book and a *Kidush* cup contributed by Bialystok Jews in Israel in 1989.

In the synagogue's entrance hall you can purchase books, guidebooks, postcards, and small souvenirs before moving on to the other museum building (also part of the synagogue complex), where you can enjoy a cup of coffee or tea and a snack. Before leaving the synagogue itself, be sure to write in its memorial book and examine the small photographic exhibit depicting the synagogue prior to 1939 and before its postwar renovations.

## House of Prayer

Next to the main synagogue, along the same narrow Kozia Street, stands a late 18th-century structure that was once designated for religious study and prayer and today functions as an annex to the synagogue museum. It is devoted to small-town life, and under its double-layered roof you will find prewar furniture, clothing,

*Tykocin: (above) Jewish cemetery in winter; (below) detail of tombstone inscription (photos TW, 1989, 1987)*

and home archives . There are also a number of paintings by Zygmunt Bujnowski (1895-1927)—an artist affiliated with the area—many of which depict life in prewar Tykocin. As you make your way through the museum, you will find yourself in the midst of an authentic prewar pharmacy, with all of its equipment miraculously intact. On the counter is an open notebook with prescriptions; next to it lies a pen, as if set aside momentarily. The names in the notebook are Polish, Jewish . . .

The activities of Tykocin's Synagogue Museum encompass more than just its permanent and changing exhibits. The museum brings cantors in to sing and sponsors concerts of Jewish music, historical lectures, and theatrical performances. You may even stumble upon a performance by the amateur theater company that Father Lech Luba of Tykocin established there in 1985. Later led by Jolanta Halecka and today under the direction of Ewa Wroczynska, the company combines the traditions of prewar Christian and Jewish performances, using a variety of Tykocin residents—teachers, farmers, students, children, and museum staff—as its players. With about two weeks' notice, the company can arrange performances for groups of 25 or more (telephone Tykocin 21473 or 181626).

As you retrace your steps back towards the synagogue, turn right at the first cross street, pass the synagogue on your left, and after about 100 meters you will come to a small wooden house still adorned with a *Magen David* (Star of David) above a front window.

## Jewish Cemetery

After leaving the synagogue, you will follow Pilsudskiego Street toward the Jewish cemetery—a short walk that will provide you with some time to reflect. Perhaps ages ago Rebeka Tyktiner followed this same route deep in thought, or that other great Jewish poet Chaim Siemiatycki (born in 1908 in Tykocin), who received the prestigious Perec Award in 1939 from the Jewish section of Warsaw's PEN Club.

As you continue down the street an uneven stretch of land will come into view, and you will begin to spot *mazevas* jutting out from the earth—450 of them in all—until you come to the northern boundary of the burial site, where an old wall seems to separate the cemetery from the nearby river. The words of the 1522 privilege of the nobleman Olbracht Gasztold for the nine Jewish families come to mind: "The place to bury their dead was provided behind the gardens, toward the forest . . . by the river." (Abram Gawurin, *Dzieje Zydow Tykocina* [History of the Jews from Tykocin] 1522-1795, Warsaw 1938.)

Not nearly as well known as the town synagogue, the Tykocin cemetery—which from the 17th century to the 20th was tended by the Holy Burial Brotherhood *Hewre Kadisza*—is one of the oldest (if not *the* oldest) of the remaining orthodox Jewish cemeteries in Poland. Although the oldest tombstone in the Tykocin cemetery dates from 1754, the first burials here took place in 1522 or soon thereafter; Jews from Bialystok were also buried here until they built their own cemetery in 1750. The cemetery in Lublin does not seem to be older despite the fact that a burial stone from that site was identified as dating from 1541 and the cemetery was mentioned in the privilege of King Sigismundus Augustus of 1555. The site for the Remuh cemetery in Kazimierz (near Cracow) was purchased by its Jewish community in 1533; however, the first burial there did not take place until 1551. And no *mazevas* are left in the Szydlow cemetery, which was established in 1470.

Visitors can obtain more information about the cemetery from the State Agency for Protection of Monuments in Bialystok (23 Dojlidy Street, tel/fax: 412332), including maps, pictures, tombstone inscription translations, and an extensive history.

## Other Tykocin Sites

This is not the end of your visit in Tykocin. Indeed its impressive baroque market square should not be missed, surrounded as it is with old wooden houses, each with its own history. The center of the market square is marked by a monument of Stefan Czarniecki, the town's former hetman. Commissioned by landowner Jan Klemens Branicki and created by French sculptor Pierre Coudray, the statue—one of the first of a secular subject in Poland—has presided over the square since 1763. In his hetman clothing, with the staff of office in his extended hand, Stefan Czarniecki has peered down upon the nearby 18th-century Holy Trinity Church for 200 years. In the eastern corner of the market, adjacent to the church and not far from the river and bridge, stands a low one-story *alumat* (seminary), which served as one of Europe's first veterans' homes (1636–1647). Between the First and Second World Wars, it served as a shelter for the region's poorest families.

From here, you will want to cross the river to visit the ruins of a 16th-century castle, the only one from that era in the Bialystok region. Visited by a number of Polish kings, including Stefan Batory (1533-86), the castle was the largest fortress in the kingdom after those in Cracow and Vilna (Vilnius) during the reign of King Batory. According to ethnographer and historian Zygmunt Gloger (1845-1910, whose tomb chapel is in the Catholic cemetery in Tykocin), the fortress was equipped with 500 cannons. Eventually, however, the castle fell into disrepair, and in 1750 its walls were partly dismantled. In 1915, Germans used the bricks to repair the road between Tykocin and Knyszyn.

For your final stop within the town proper, return to the market and venture south along the church wall on narrow Jordan Street (an area previously off-limits to Jews) to reach a Catholic monastery complex that today serves as a home for retired priests.

## Lopuchowo

### *(4 km SW of Tykocin)*

The last stop on your Tykocin trip—the Lopuchowo Forest—was the final stop for the Tykocin Jews on August 5, 1941.

On this date, under the command of special delegate Wolfgang Birkner of the Warsaw Gestapo, police units 309 and 316—"Kommando Bialystok"—together with local police drove the Tykocin Jews out of their homes and then on to Zawady, where trucks transported them to the forest near the village of Lopuchowo. There 2,000 Jewish men, women, and children were murdered. Today an obelisk commemorates this final tragic chapter in the history of Tykocin's Jewish community. It is a place to light a candle and say a *kaddish* for the dead.

# BIALYSTOK

*Population 276,045 (in 1993)*

*185 km northeast of Warsaw, via Highway 28.*

## History

In 1939, prior to the Holocaust, 84 percent of all the Jews in the world either lived in Poland, or on former Polish lands, or were descendants of Jews who had lived there. Of all the cities in the world with more than 100,000 inhabitants, Bialystok, on the eve of World War II, had the highest percentage Jewish population—over 60 percent—higher even than Poland's capital, Warsaw, or than Vilna (Vilnius), Lithuania's capital, which was referred to as "the Jerusalem of the North." Bialystok also had the greatest number of synagogues per capita. In the years between the First and Second World Wars, Bialystok was home to approximately 100 Jewish temples and *minians* (places where ten or more met to pray). Historian Abraham Samuel Herszberg (*Pinkos Bialistok*, vols. I, II, New York: 1949-1950) described 59 of these Bialystok synagogues in detail. By comparison, during a similar period Warsaw had 200 synagogues and Cracow 40. As for rabbis, in 1897, Bialystok had 33!

The table in Appendix III illustrates the dramatic growth of the Jewish population in Bialystok. In the 19th century it increased more than 60-fold, while the increase in the rapidly developing city of Lodz was only 30-fold. In Bialystok in 1895, of the population of 62,993, Jews numbered 47,783 (over 75 percent of the total). In 1912, according to *The Jewish Encyclopedia*, of 98,700 Bialystok residents, 73,950 were Jews (77 percent of the population). It was almost as large a Jewish population as in Palestine in 1922 (82,794).

In the fall of 1939, after the Russian army entered Bialystok, the Bialystok population soared from 107,000 to almost 400,000. It is estimated that 70 percent of the population was Jewish, mostly Jews who had fled the western part of Poland which had been conquered by the Germans. By the time the Germans invaded Bialystok in June 1941, the Jewish population in Bialystok was back down to between 80,000 and 120,000.

The first written mention of Bialystok is relatively recent— 1514. And it was not until 1692 that Bialystok received the royally bestowed "privileges" giving it status as a town. However, notations in the *Pinkos Bialystok* of the Tykocin *kahal* indicate that Jews were living in Bialystok as far back as 1658, when it was still considered a village. As a small group they accepted the authority of the Tykocin *kahal*. A notation from 1661 indicates that the first Jewish leaseholders in Bialystok were Jakub and Izaac Segal, sons of Moshe Segal.

By 1663, the Jewish settlement in Bialystok and its immediate surroundings numbered 75 women and men over the age of 14. Thirty years later a *subkahal* was established, with its own house of prayer.

From 1715 to 1718, Bialystok Jews built a new brick synagogue on the site of an earlier wooden synagogue. This structure stood until 1941. Jan Klemens Branicki, the owner of the town at the time of the synagogue's construction, contributed significantly to the settlement of Jews in Bialystok by granting them legal privileges at the beginning of the 18th century and giving them financial assistance to build the synagogue. In addition, he allowed the Jewish community to participate in the town elections of 1749. Bialystok's subsequent owner, Branicki's widow, Izabela Branicka, confirmed these privileges and issued a number of instructions, obligations, and restrictions concerning Jewish inhabitants. Among them was the decree that the rabbi "should not grant marriage to those Jews who have no means for making a living."

In the 18th century, Bialystok's Jewish district—with all of its administrative institutions (synagogue, rabbi's office, hospital, and cemetery)—occupied the northwestern portion of the town. As that century progressed, the community became more and more independent of the Tykocin *kahal*, as indicated by the completion of a second brick synagogue in 1765. In that same year, 761 Jews inhabited Bialystok and the nearby villages. By 1799 (as indicated by a Prussian census), 1,788 of Bialystok's 3,930 residents were Jews. From this point until 1941, Jews represented the largest religious group in town, reaching a peak at the turn of the 20th century when they numbered approximately 50,000, and

then again at the beginning of the city's Soviet occupation in
October and November 1939.

In 1882, the Chovevei Zion party (Lovers of Zion)—one of the
first Jewish parties to promote the Zionist movement—was organized in Bialystok. In 1897 the working-class Bund party came
into being, accompanied by the Yiddish newspaper *Bialystoker
Arbeiter*. In addition, there existed Agudath Israel and the Jewish
People's Party, both powerful political parties. Sports clubs
included Maccabi, Hapoel, Hakoach, and youth organizations

such as Haszomir Hacair, Dror, and
others.

In 1889, a fire brigade 90 percent
comprised of Jews was formed, and in
1913 Nachum Cemach organized the
famous Jewish Hebrew Habimah theater in Bialystok. By the 1920s, numerous charitable, medical, and social organizations existed, including Bikur
Cholim, and Gemillus Chasodim, which
later became the famous Linas
Hatsedek emergency service. In addition, Bialystok's many schools, hospitals, shelters, homes for the aged, and
"kitchens" for the poor caused it to
become known among European Jews
as "The City with the Golden Heart."

*Bialystok: The Jewish quar-
ter, c. 1934 (photo E.
Kazimirowski, collection TW)*

In 1912, shortly before World War I,
75 percent of the town's 98,700 residents were Jews (73,950).
However, in the years between World War I and World War II,
that percentage declined as Jews began to emigrate overseas—to
the United States and, to a lesser degree, Palestine. However, in
Bialystok, no anti-Jewish incidents took place after the infamous
1906 pogrom which had been provoked by the Russian army.
Compared to Vilnius, Warsaw, and Lvov, Bialystok was a relatively peaceful place for Jews. In a 1937 boxing match, Aron
Brzezinski, a fighter from the Jewish club Maccabi Bialystok,
delivered a blow to his opponent from Jagiellonia, Zdanowicz,
that caused him to lose consciousness and then die despite doctors' best efforts to revive him. Such an event would have caused
riots in cities with anti-Semitic traditions; Bialystok, however,
remained calm.

At the outbreak of World War II, Bialystok fell under Soviet rule and thus became a haven for Jews fleeing Nazi-conquered areas. At this point the population of Bialystok grew from 107,000 to 250,000, and then in November 1939 to nearly 400,000, made up predominantly of Jews who had escaped east from Warsaw, Lodz, and the other cities in "Generalna Gubernia," the German-occupied portion of Poland. In June 1940, some refugees—especially Poles (non-Jews)—began returning to German-occupied areas. Although no precise data exists, it is believed that at this time Jews numbered more than 250,000 in Bialystok—without a doubt, one of the world's largest concentrations of Jews, after Warsaw and Lodz.

During the Soviet occupation most of Bialystok's synagogues were used for food storage, cinemas, and small sweatshops. One example was the butchers' synagogue, Kacowiszer Beth Midrash, on Zamenhofa Street, which was converted to an arts workshop where posters, banners, and other Communist propaganda materials were made.

*Pietrasze Forest Memorial, with explanatory sign in foreground (photo DHE, 1993)*

At 6 p.m. on Friday, June 27, 1941, Field Marshal Fedor von Bock and General Heinz Guderian led the German army into Bialystok. On the first day of their occupation there was a pogrom in which the Great Synagogue and the surrounding area were burned. In the first big roundup, on July 11, the Germans took 4,000 men and boys to the Pietrasze Forest and shot them (see photo). On August 1, 1941, they established the Jewish quarters—the Bialystok ghetto—to house between 40,000 and 55,000 Jews from Bialystok and other towns in the region.

Spurred by the ghetto's prison-like conditions—crowded, unsanitary, and consistently low on food—and their growing recognition of what lay ahead, in 1942 the ghetto's inhabitants (especially the youth) began to organize a resistance movement.

Jakub Rywkind, a member of the underground who was a mathematician at Vilnius University before the war, offered this laconic summation of ghetto life: "We are all the dead on a holiday." Unable to tolerate living in this way any longer, on Sunday night, August 15, 1943, a number of ghetto residents decided to offer armed resistance despite the three rings of German soldiers and police surrounding the ghetto.

Within the ghetto, the Organization of Jewish Self-Defense was passing around the manifesto: "Don't be lambs for slaughter! Fight for your life to the last breath . . . Remember the example and tradition of numerous generations of Jewish fighters, martyrs, thinkers and builders, pioneers, and creators. Come out to the streets and fight!"

That call was answered. Two days later, on August 17, Bialystok looked like a city under siege. All traffic had stopped. Armed vehicles stood at the city's exits. The ghetto was burning. More than 200 armed Jewish fighters were estimated to be within Bialystok's borders. To stop the fighting—which lasted for six days—the Germans used tanks, artillery, and airplanes. The ghetto's own defense was the biggest battle in the city. Unofficial data and eyewitness accounts put the Nazi losses at 100 soldiers killed or wounded. As for the Jews, only those who escaped into the forests, hid on the Aryan side, or jumped off the extermination camp-bound trains survived. The rest were murdered in the gas chambers of Majdanek or Treblinka. Historian Szymon Datner estimates that 200,000 Jews from the Bialystok region were murdered, 60,000 of them taken from the Bialystok ghetto.

In 1945 about 1,085 Jews came to Bialystok, 260 of whom had survived the ghetto by hiding either within its confines or in the surrounding area. For two to three years, two synagogues continued to function, one on Polna Street (Cytron Beth Midrash) and another on Piekna (Piaskower Beth Midrash). Most of the few Jews who were left emigrated after 1968, following an anti-semitic campaign provoked by the Communist regime. Today, only a few remain.

World War II saw not only the total annihilation of the Jewish community in Bialystok, but 80 percent of the city as well. After the war, however a new city was quick to develop. With more than 280,000 residents today, the city is home to a medical university, the Polytechnic University, Bialystok University, the Warsaw Academy of Music, and the Warsaw Theater Academy. In addi-

*Bialystok: 50th anniversary commemoration of Jewish ghetto resistance, Zabia Street cemetery site, August 1993. (above) Archbishop Stanislaw Szymecki talking with Rabbi Josif Gliksberg from Israel. (below left) some of the Bialystoker Jews from around the world who attended the ceremony. (right) Polish guard at the memorial to resistance fighters (photos TW, 1993)*

tion, the city boasts two theaters, a philharmonic orchestra, museums, and art galleries, as well as a growing light industry sector, particularly in textiles and electronics.

## A Walk Through Bialystok

We are assuming that most visitors will want to stay at least a day and night in Bialystok; however, for those who wish only to stay a few hours, we offer shorter sightseeing options at the end of this chapter. (See key to city map in Appendix X.)

After checking into one of the city's several hotels—all of which offer single and double rooms, hot water, TV, telephone, and restaurants—you will be ready to walk around the downtown. There's no point driving unless you are staying on the outskirts of the city. There are several guarded parking lots.

Guided by the map on page 146, begin near the old town hall, which was constructed between 1745 and 1761 and today houses the "regional" art museum. Prior to World War II, the town hall was home to more than a hundred Jewish shops as well as an observation point for the fire brigade. Next to it was a bus depot. It was here in nearby stores that the famous *bialy* roll—round with onions and poppyseeds—could be purchased. (Today you'd be lucky to find this roll is Bialystok, but it is popular in many cities in the United States and Israel.) Recently, a monument to Marshal Jozef Pilsudski (1867-1935) was erected on the western side of the town hall square. Pilsudski was a heroic commander of the Polish Army between the two world wars and was President of Poland from 1918 to 1922 and Premier 1926-28, 1930.

*Town Hall to 26 Zamenhofa Street (10 minutes to walk there)*

As you exit northeast from the square and cross Lipowa Street, you will turn toward the narrow Zamenhofa Street. Once lively and noisy, this street was called *Jatke Gas* because of the many Jewish meat stores there. After you pass a single wooden house (on the east side, on your right) and come to the end of the street, you will find yourself in front of a multistory building (26 Zamenhofa) with a commemorative plaque recalling in Polish and Esperanto that here, on the then Zielona Street (*Grin Gas*), Lejzor Ludwik Zamenhof, the creator of Esperanto, was born on December 15, 1859. He died in 1917. The house where he was born—and which stood until several years after the war—was

actually situated slightly higher than the surviving wooden structure (see photos below). While standing here, imagine for a
moment the Bialystok of the second half of the 19th century—a
town whose inhabitants spoke in their own hybrid languages of
Yiddish, Byelorussian, Russian, Polish, and German. It's difficult
to imagine more suitable field experience for the future linguist
and creator of the most successful artificial universal language.

*Zamenhofa Street to 10 Malmeda Street (5 minutes)*

Returning southwest along the same street, you will turn
right after about 100 meters and go through a gate and straight
ahead about 25 meters. You will now be on Piotrkowska Street.
Known as Kupiecka (Merchant) Street before the war, this street
was noteworthy for its printing offices and restaurants.
Semiprofessional musicians were always at the ready to entertain
restaurant patrons; in fact, some of the most passionate ones were

**Bialystok:** *(above) Esperantists gather in 1929 at birthplace of Ludwik
Zamenhof (photo Josif Giladi, courtesy of J. Giladi). (below) plaque at site of
birthplace, Zamenhofa Street (photo TW, 1994)*

the restaurant owners themselves. Recalled Kalman Kania, a
Bialystok Jewish resident until his death in 1993: "A fiddle would
hang next to a hat on the coat stand. Guests came—some to play
chess, others to play music."

Straight ahead on Piotrkowska
Street will lead you to Malmeda
Street. At the intersection of
Pietrowska and Malmeda Streets, on
your right is a stone building (10
Malmeda Street) with a black marble
plaque. The plaque identifies the
spot—in what used to be the
Bialystok ghetto—where a heroic
Jewish fighter, Icchok Malmed, was
executed by hanging on February 8,
1943 (see photo). He had thrown acid
in the faces of some marauding Nazi
soldiers. He gave himself up when
the Germans threatened to retaliate
by shooting 1,000 Jews.

After the ghetto uprising, the
neighborhood was completely
destroyed; thus, all of the buildings
you see along Malmeda Street today
date from after the war. This area

*Bialystok: plaque on Malmeda
Street in memory of Icchok
Malmed, hero in Jewish ghetto
resistance (photo TW, 1993)*

also served as home—on a small street called Rozanska—to the
Jewish medical service Linas Hatsedek (LH), or literally, "on duty
for the sick." Formed in 1885, the organization grew out of the
uproar aroused in the Jewish community by the death of the doctor Mejer Shohet, who fell ill and because he lived alone escaped
the notice of the community. The first society of its type in
Europe, LH provided timely medical assistance to anyone who
needed it, without regard to nationality, religion, or social position, giving rise to the familiar expression of the time: "As fast as
a Linas Hatsedek ambulance." It was not until several years later
that similar organizations sprang up in Russia and other parts of
Poland (in 1901 in Warsaw).

The residents of Bialystok valued the activities of the LH—
such as the night-long vigils at the bedsides of the sick and lonely
by members of the LH Brotherhood—and the town authorities
provided financial support until the society's tragic end on

August 16, 1943, when the liquidation began of the entire Jewish
district and its inhabitants following the ghetto uprising.

*Malmeda Street to the Zamenhof Monument (5 minutes)*

Walking southwest on Malmeda Street (back towards the
town center), you will reach a small square park bordered by
Malmeda, Bialowny, and Spoldzielcza streets. In the middle of the
square stands a statue of Ludwik Zamenhof, the creator of
Esperanto. He was born in 1859 in Bialystok. As you continue up
Malmeda Street, you will pass on the left an entrance to the narrow street, Bialowny. This small street that forms the southern
border of the square was called in Polish "Zydowska," or Jewish
Street, before the war. From Malmeda, you will make your way
back to the city's main street, Lipowa, where in August 1941 the
main wooden gate to the Jewish quarter—the gate to the ghetto—
was constructed.

*Bialowna to 33 Lipowa Street (5 minutes)*

When you reach Lipowa Street, turn right and walk in the
direction of the "white church," built during the two decades
between 1928 and 1947. If you cross Lipowa Street as you make
your way from Malmeda, you will encounter the mid-19th century Orthodox St. Nicolaus Church. If you continue on another half-
kilometer, you will come to an antiquarian bookstore worth
exploring (at 18 Lipowa Street). Inside you might find some old
Hebrew and Yiddish books. On the other side of Lipowa Street
once again, retrace your steps for a few meters and you will find
yourself in front of a building (at 33 Lipowa Street) with a plaque
commemorating Jakub Szapiro. Szapiro was before the Second
World War the leader of Bialystok's Esperanto followers as well as
an outstanding historian, journalist, writer and teacher. He was
killed by the Nazis in 1943 in the Pietrasze forest.

Szapiro wrote the first published guidebook of Bialystok in
1923, which was printed in Esperanto. In the introduction to
*Gvidilo tra Bialystok, la Naskurba de la Majstro* ("Guide to Bialystok,
Birthplace of the Master") Szapiro wrote: "Bialystok, where our
master [Zamenhof] was born and spent his youth, is little known
to followers of Esperanto all over the world. Hence the purpose of
this guidebook is to familiarize them with this city." The guide-

**Bialystok:** *Two views of ul. Lipowa, the main street. (above) Looking east, late 19th century (from photo in Alfons Karny Sculpture Museum. (below) In 1917 (postcard in collection TW)*

book even contained logos of companies whose owners stated their willingness to correspond in Esperanto.

The plaque honoring Szapiro was placed in July 1991, and among those at the ceremony was Felicja Nowak, a niece of Szapiro. She had spent time in the Bialystok ghetto and survived the Holocaust by hiding in the countryside. Her reminiscences of that time are contained in her book *Moja Gwiazda* ("My Star"), published in Poland in 1992.

*33 Lipowa Street to the Jewish School of Handicrafts (5 minutes)*

Walk west once again towards the "white church" until you reach the secession-style building at 35 Lipowa Street. It was built by the wealthy Jewish Nowik family. Turn left (south) and you quickly will find yourself in front of the two-story building (on the right) that presently houses the physics department of the Bialystok branch of the University of Warsaw. Until 1939, this building was home to the Jewish School of Handicrafts, which was named after the well-known Jewish philanthropist and industrialist M. W. Wysocki (41 Lipowa St.). Further up the hill at 41 D Lipowa you will come across a brick building that before World War II served as a Jewish Artisan's school founded by the ORT organization (Society of Jewish Workers). It was built at the beginning of the 20th century. The building also contained the rabbi's office as well as a small prayer hall. In the rear of the building, you can still detect details characteristic of Jewish architecture, such as high windows typical in synagogues.

*Old Barbican Mission*

You may wish to detour to the complex of buildings—at 23 Swiety Rocha Street—that served until 1939 as the seat of the Barbican Mission, which was established to convert Jews to Protestantism. Financed by its London headquarters, the mission in Bialystok was part of the largest organization of its kind in Europe and included a church (now the "Syrena" movie house), printing office, library, and outpatient clinic. Despite the size of its operations, the mission had only limited success—not only in Bialystok but in the cities of Grodno, Vilna, and Rowne as well. According to its own records, the mission could only claim one hundred Jewish converts. And the converts of Jewish heritage met with the same fate as their Jewish brethren during the Holocaust. They were placed in the ghetto where they were killed, along with their leader, Parson Piotr Gorodiszcz.

*Puppet Theater, Park, Mazeva (5 minutes)*

If you continue south, straight ahead between blocks of flats, you will reach Kalinowskiego Street. On the far side of the street you will see a modern complex of buildings, which house the Puppet Theater. Crossing the street, follow an asphalt path that runs between the theater and park. Opposite the entrance to the theater you may see a lone *mazeva*, which serves as the only reminder of the Jewish cemetery that earlier occupied the site of this current city park.

Founded in 1752, the cemetery here was closed in 1890 when a new cemetery was opened on Wschodnia Street in the district of Bagnowka. Prior to World War II, the cemetery was surrounded by a stone wall; however, after the Nazis entered Bialystok in 1941, much of the cemetery was systematically destroyed. Although a portion of it survived the war, postwar communist authorities decided to destroy the entire cemetery. Remaining tombstones were covered with the soil cleared for constructing the nearby Communist Party committee building that today houses one of the University of Warsaw buildings (on the roundabout at the intersection of Suraska, Liniarskiego and Marie Sklodwskiej Curie Streets). It's likely that a number of *mazevas* remain buried under the park (see 1930 photo below).

*Bialystok: 1930 view of tombstones in the oldest Jewish cemetery, no longer in existence (photo Jan Glinka; courtesy Osrodek Dokumentacji Zabytkow (ODZ), Warsaw)*

Shortly before World War II, Polish historian Jan Glinka described the cemetery as follows (based on records in the Bialystok Municipality Archive, Rynek Kosciuszki 4): "From the entrance gate southward, parallel to Minska Street, across the whole cemetery is a row of tombs of rabbis and other important Jews. Next to the gate, at the foot of the hill, is the grave of Rabbi Kalman. The inscription on the stone has his name, the name of his father, Mojzesz Josef, the fact that he ran a higher rabbinical school, and the year of his death, 1789. In the same row of graves but more toward the interior of the cemetery where the hill begins to descend is the grave of Izaak Zabludowski who died in 1865. His tombstone is made of four plates, each richly covered with bas reliefs in the Empire and rococo styles and representing buildings he founded: the synagogue on Zydowska Street and the Jewish hospital . . . " This hospital survived and is at 15 Warszawska Street.

*Marketplace, 3 Piekna Street (10 minutes)*

As you continue south, you will pass the amphitheater on your right and see a small 18th-century Russian Orthodox chapel behind the hill. On narrow Odeska Street you will enter the old Sienny market, which is still surrounded by some former Jewish homes dating from before World War I.

If you proceed from the market and turn right on Piekna Street, you will come to a 19th-century, though newly renovated, building that currently functions as the restaurant "Premiera." Across the street, adjacent to the bank, at 3 Piekna Street stands the old synagogue building "Piaskower Beth Midrash," itself on a site formerly inhabited by a wooden synagogue completed in 1821. By the middle of the 19th century, however, the wooden structure had already become dilapidated and a committee had been formed to collect funds for a new house of prayer. It was built in 1890 with the help of a subvention from members of the committee: D. Ostrynski, J. Rozental, E. Slobocki, C. Wilsztyk, M.

Wilmer, and C. Mazewis. However, the main support came from Icchok Jaczmienik, Israel Kaltun, Malka Nawiaska and industrialist Mojzesz Nowik.

With its own sewage system and electric lighting, the new synagogue was quite modern for its time. Visitors were particularly surprised by the unusually bright light emanating from its 73 electric lamps. The poor prayed at long tables because the places along the eastern wall of the synagogue were actually purchased and reserved before the syn-

**Bialystok:** *former synagogue on Piekna Street, now offices for a construction firm and Zamenhof Esperanto Society and tourist center (photo DHE, 1993). Plaque on wall memorializes use as synagogue (photo TW, 1995)*

agogue's construction in a sort of no-interest loan arrangement typical of synagogue construction at the time. The building survived the war and in the 1950s this place of worship became the "Pioneer " movie house and also served as headquarters for the Bialystok Division of the Jewish Social and Cultural Society. In the 1970s it was used as a community cultural center before falling into neglect. In 1991, after a fire destroyed the roof, a renovation was begun which was completed in 1995 (see photo). The building will house the Ludwik Zamenhof Foundation office and tourist information center as well as the offices of a construction company. There is a commemorative plaque on the building stating its history as a synagogue prior to World War II (see photo). If you look closely at the building, you will see, at its rear, the characteristic high, half-rounded windows of the main prayer hall.

*The Burned Great Synagogue, 1 Suraska Street (10 minutes)*

After finishing your meal at Premiera, you can follow Mlynowa Street east, and then Suraska Street (northeast) back to the city center. On your left at the roundabout, on the edge of the park is a large monument to the September 1939 defenders of Bialystok. (Approximately 38,000 Jews served in the Polish Army during World War II, the highest percentage of any army in the world.)

Continuing down Suraska Street, a short block beyond the roundabout, turn right (south) into a driveway. In this area until 1941 stood the Great Synagogue. On the south wall of the new building is a plaque in Polish and Yiddish commemorating the "3,000 Jewish martyrs burned alive in the Great Synagogue in Bialystok by the Nazi murderers on 24 June, 1941" (see photo next page). Placed there on August 16, 1958—the fifteenth anniversary of the ghetto uprising—the plaque unfortunately contains some errors: The synagogue was set ablaze on June 27, not June 24, and those who died in the fire, which included the elderly, women, and children, numbered approximately 800 rather than 3,000. In August 1995, in a ceremony celebrating the 50th anniversary of the end of World War II, a new and handsome sculpture and monument was dedicated in a small square nearby—in memory of those killed in the synagogue (see photos page 51).

***Bialystok:*** *plaque on Suraska Street memorializing victims of Great Synagogue burning in 1941 (photo TW, 1994)*

Built between 1908 and 1913, the Great Synagogue was designed by architect Szlojme Jakow Rabinowicz, father of the famous religious painter Ben Cijon Rabinowicz, who was known in Paris under the pseudonym "Benn." Topped by a large dome with a spire of about ten meters, the synagogue also featured two smaller symmetrical decorative domes atop its side halls. Under the main dome—which was supported by steel and concrete pillars that at the lower level were incorporated in the *bimah*'s construction—the indoor lighting system included eight small windows (*lukarnas*). The synagogue's 20th-century construction was especially impressive in the way it incorporated three domes into the regular structure of the cuboid. As was characteristic of the time, the synagogue employed a mixture of architectural styles—primarily neo-Gothic and Byzantine. Characteristic of many synagogues built at the beginning of the 20th century, the structure's dome exhibited a Byzantine-Muslim influence in an attempt to reduce the neo-Gothic appearance that had become so closely identified with Christianity (see photo below).

At the synagogue—which was only open on Saturdays and holidays—women prayed together with men, though in separate halls that surrounded the main prayer hall on three sides (the fourth, or eastern side, was occupied by the Ark). Such 20th-century novelties as choir and organ were introduced, and during the period

***Bialystok:*** *the Great Synagogue in 1922 (photographer unknown; collection TW)*

between World War I and World War II, national holidays were celebrated with services attended by such city authorities as the mayor and the governor of the region. The last official rabbi of Bialystok, Dr. Gedali Rozenman, at the end of the prayer and Jewish hymn "*Hatikve*" would intone the Polish national anthem "Jeszcze Polska nie zginela."

The Great Synagogue's size and prestige attracted cantors from all over Poland, as well as from neighboring countries. In 1934 for the *Pesach* holiday, as many as 14 cantors offered their services to the governing board of the synagogue.

## Bialystok by Auto

*City Center to Branicki Palace*

Having left your car on Lipowa Street, you will again begin your tour downtown, this time driving east. At the intersection of Lipowa and Sienkiewicza streets, you will pass by the oldest part of the city on your left. On the far left, at the northeast corner, you will see an 18th-century building that currently houses the Astoria restaurant. Prior to World War II it was the Jewish drugstore Anna Halaj.

Further down Lipowa Street (at this point its name has changed to "Rynek Kosciuszki"), on the left you will see the low red-roofed building that contains the regional archives. Across the street (and adorned by pillars) is the 250-year-old Sisters of Mercy cloister. Also on your left, you will catch sight of the top of a tall red neo-Gothic Catholic cathedral built in the early 1900s. Sharing a fragment of its wall is a small white Catholic church dating from 1617, the oldest building in the city. Just behind the small church you will find an 18th-century parish house. On the main street, past the cathedral, you will encounter the present Central Library, which is housed in the building where the Free Mason "Golden Ring" (Masonic Lodge) was once based.

Branicki Park is now on your right. The Branicki family were the owners of Bialystok in the 17th and 18th centuries and the city grew up in this immediate area around their park and palace. In Branicki Park close to the roadway you'll see a tall, black statue of Father Jerzy Popieluszko. He was a popular Catholic priest in Warsaw in the 1970s and early 1980s. He was an active and publicly vocal communist resister and was brutally murdered by secret agents of the Polish Communist regime in 1984.

**Bialystok:** *ceremony dedicating monument to victims of Great Synagogue burning, held in August 1995, 50 years after end of World War II. (above) view of the monument and some of many participants from abroad. (below, left) Meier Zawadzki, a Bialystoker Jew now living in Haifa. (right) Michael Flikier, head of the Society of Bialystoker Jews in Israel (photos TW, 1995)*

*Bialystok: Branicki Palace gate (photo DHE, 1993)*

Ahead on your right (about 100 meters) you'll reach the Branicki Palace gate. Turn sharp right and drive into the large courtyard. It was here that Jan Klemens Branicki gave "privileges" to Bialystok Jews, encouraging them to settle in the area. This baroque palace dates from the 17th century and its parks and ponds once covered many acres and extended more than a half mile to the south. The palace was heavily damaged in World War II, was reconstructed and is now part of a medical university ("Medical Academy"). Its main rooms are sometimes open to the public and the large upstairs ballroom (*aula*) is particularly attractive. There is also a pleasant view overlooking the gardens from the upper balcony. Enjoy a walk in the French-style gardens adorned with baroque sculptures. At the far end of the gardens, a brick bridge will take you across a large pond.

*The Ritz Hotel*

After leaving the palace grounds the same way you entered, drive straight towards the small bridge that spans the Biala River and towards the roundabout with Aleja Pilsudskiego. Before World War II, you would have found yourself in front of Bialystok's famous Ritz Hotel, which some considered the town's primary attraction. It was certainly the most elegant and comfort-

*Bialystok: the Ritz Hotel in 1927; built by Jewish interests, it is no longer standing (photographer unknown; collection TW)*

able hotel in the provincial towns of the formerly Russian-governed area of Poland. Bialystok's Ritz was built by Mitia Rubinsztejn, father of Siergiej Rubinsztejn (1889-1960), a well-regarded professor of psychology and philosophy at Moscow University in the period between the two world wars. The Ritz was owned by the Jewish company Rabmil (Rabinowicz and Milejkowski) and operated by the same people who ran London's famous Ritz Hotel. Just behind the hotel stood the Palace, a Jewish theater built in 1912. The 900-seat theater, which boasted central heating, hosted such performers as poet Julian Tuwim and writer Ilya Ehrenburg, as well as such popular Jewish theater companies as Sniegov's "Mozaika Hall" and the Warsaw "Azazel", with famous stars of Jewish Theater in Poland before World War II such as Ajzyk Somberg, Jonas Turkow, and Ida Kaminska. Today, however, the Ritz and the Palace theater are gone. Both were destroyed by the Nazis.

*A Star of David on Warszawska Street*

To continue your journey, circle the roundabout halfway, proceed a block and turn right (in a southerly direction) onto Warszawska Street . After about a block, you will see a red Catholic church on your right, which functioned as a Lutheran church before World War II. Adjacent to this structure, at 50 Warszawska, is a 19th-century apart-ment house on which an iron Star of David has been preserved on a wall

**Bialystok:** *Star of David on apartment house on Warszawska Street (photo DHE, 1993)*

overhanging the sidewalk (see photo). Shingles with six-point stars hung from many Jewish houses. You can view a similar one in the courtyard of another former Jewish home at 14 Sienkiewicza Street, which is now used by the Theater School.

*School of Trade for Men*

Across the street, at 63 Warszawska Street, you will see a large building with columns in front. It was here in 1900 that a group of Jewish industrialists converted an old building into the School of Trade for Men . It is now used as a branch of Bialystok University.

*Synagogue at Branickiego Street*

From here, you will continue on for several meters before
turning right onto Swietojanska Street. After driving down a
slight hill, you will turn right again onto Branickiego Street. On
your left, you will pass a Belgian-built power plant dating from
the end of the 19th century, and behind it and among the trees
you will be able to make out the City Theater, which was built in
1935. Before reaching the roundabout (which you drove around
previously), park the car and walk towards a gray building on
your right at 3 Branickiego. This is the former synagogue.

Despite several aborted attempts (dating from 1866) and resistance from czarist authorities—who wanted to construct their
own Orthodox church on the site and were also concerned about
its proximity to the elite school for young Christian ladies (i.e.,
daughters of the nobility) in the nearby Branicki Palace—Szmuel
Beth Midrash was finally built in 1902 and immediately declared
to be the most beautiful synagogue in the city. Named after
Szmuel Mohilever—a famous rabbi, Zionist and friend of
Theodor Herzl, the creator of Zionist ideology—who died in
Bialystok in 1896, "Szmuel's House" had a particularly impressive
facade, distinguished by its neo-byzantine style. Although the
synagogue was destroyed during World War II, it was partially
rebuilt after the war, serving first as a movie house and now as a
sports hall. If you look at the back of the structure, you will still
be able to detect some characteristic Jewish architectural details
such as the high half-rounded windows and a small apse. In 1992
a plaque describing the building's earlier use (in Polish and
Hebrew) was placed on the front of the structure.

*Jewish Maternity Hospital*

Back in your car, turn right again at the roundabout and then
go left on Warszawska Street. To your immediate right (at No. 15)
is a white, two-story building that formerly housed a Jewish
maternity hospital and continues to serve as a maternity hospital
today. Founded in 1863, this is the same hospital pictured on the
tombstone of Isaac Zabludowski (see earlier description of the
cemetery, page 46). In fact, the hospital carried Zabludowski's
name until 1939. A plaque recently unearthed in the basement of
the building indicates that the hospital was renovated between

1936 and 1938. Both the mayor of Bialystok and the governor of the region, in addition to the Jewish community, supported the renovation. Dr. Owadia Kaplan was the hospital's director at the time of its renovation. Others who worked there included Dr. Mojzesz Perelsztejn, Dr. Aleksander Rajgrodzki (vice mayor of Bialystok), and Dr. Abraham Kniaziew. The hospital is the oldest in Bialystok.

As you continue on, passing several large residences, you will not be surprised to learn that Warszawska Street was home primarily to the city's wealthy. On your left behind a low brick wall (at No. 8), one of the best secondary schools in Bialystok— Gymnasium of King Zygmunt August—will come into view. Ludwik Zamenhof was a pupil here and a brass plaque on the wall indicating that can be seen from the car.

*Jewish Cemetery*

At the end of Warszawska Street, turn right onto Sienkiewicza Street and then right again after the underpass at the first major intersection. You will find yourself near a small, forested park that's home to a Lutheran cemetery dating from the 1890s. As you continue on this road (towards "Sokolka and Grodno"), watch for an intersection in which the street forks into two main roads—the left heading toward Sokolka and the right to Suprasl. Turn right onto Wschodnia Street just before you reach this intersection, and then continue on this rough road for about 500 meters until you see the brick wall on the left that surrounds the Jewish cemetery.

You have now reached the largest Jewish cemetery in Northern Poland. Within its 12-hectare (or approximately 30-acre) boundaries are nearly 7,000 *mazevas*, a fraction of the approximately 35-40,000 that vied for space here before the occupying Germans removed them to build sidewalks, roads, and even buildings during the time of the Holocaust. Like the adjacent Catholic and Russian Orthodox cemetery, the Jewish burial site was founded about 1890. The first person buried here was probably "a woman Fruma, daughter of Jehuda Lejb, dead in 5652 (1892)", or so translates the inscription on her *mazeva*. The last burial here occurred in 1969. Most of the inscriptions are in Hebrew, though there are also some in Yiddish, Russian, German, English and Polish.

After you pass through the gate, walk straight ahead until
you reach a striking tomb that resembles a house with a conical
roof. This *ohel* (shelter around a tomb)—the gift of Bialystok Jews
then living in New York—was built in 1922 in memory of Rabbi
Chaim Herc Halpern, son of *Gaon* Rabbi Lipe Lepele. Halpern
was Chief Rabbi of Bialystok for more than 50 years and highly
respected in the community until his death in 1919. Next to his
*ohel* was that of Rabbi Szmuel Mohilever, whose remains were
exhumed by his family in 1991 and taken to Israel.

If you turn right at Rabbi Halpern's *ohel,* you will see a large
black marble pillar commemorating the victims of the Jewish
pogrom in Bialystok in June 1906. The pillar is inscribed with the
names of the approximately 110 Jews who were murdered on this
day (the names are listed in the *Memory Book of Bialystok*, New
York, 1982, p. 18), as well as the following epitaph, written by the
famous Hebrew poet Zalman Schneur:

*Pillar of Sorrow: Stand strong and be proud, you pillar of sorrow*
*Like marble melt not in the blood of the holy martyrs beneath you*
*Nor dissolve into a flood of tears.*
*Even as states and people change, never move from your place*
*Strike fear into them at night, hover over them like a curse*
*A cold witness shall you be,*
*telling what occurred to the children who come after us.*
*    For the honor and the blood of our people were defiled,*
*as witnessed by the summer heavens. The sun shone unabashed;*
*the eyes of the world were not blinded.*

*Hebrew Gymnasium*

As you return to town after visiting the cemetery, you will
drive through a tunnel and then past a traffic light. After another
150 meters, turn right into a drive that will take you to the yard of
the Polish Red Cross (PCK) Hospital at 79 Sienkiewicza Street.
Prior to World War II, this building was home to the co-educa-
tional Hebrew Gymnasium, the leading Jewish school in Bialystok
and one of the best secondary schools in Poland. Begun in 1920, it
was only 15 years later that the school's board of directors decided to build a larger building and this is the same building that is
still standing today (see photo on next page). In 1990 the school's

former students celebrated its 70th anniversary with a reunion in Haifa, Israel. Yitzhak Shamir, a graduate of the school and then Prime Minister of Israel, presided over the festivities' opening. In 1993 a plaque (in Hebrew and Polish) was placed at the entrance to the hospital describing its former existence as a Jewish school (see photo).

*Bialystok: Hebrew Gymnasium on Sienkiewicza Street before World War II; now used as a hospital (photographer unknown; collection TW)*

*The Ghetto Cemetery at Zabia Street*

Proceeding along Sienkiewicza, you will cross the Biala River and then turn right onto the wide street Aleja Jozefa Pilsudskiego and then right again (after about 800 meters and near the "PKO" Bank) onto the short street Bohaterow Getta. Finally, you will turn left onto Zabia Street,

where you will find a small park on your right. Here, among the trees, you will see a 12-foot high monument decorated with the Star of David commemorating the leaders and fighters of the Bialystok ghetto uprising. Nearby and surrounded by an iron fence is an obelisk commemorating the 3,000 Jews murdered in the Bialystok ghetto. Both are on the site of the former ghetto cemetery. Tended by the Holy Brotherhood of Burials *Hewre Kadisza*, this Bialystok cemetery was the only ghetto cemetery in Europe.

After World War II, about 1,100 Jews came to Bialystok to live, approximately 900 of whom were former inhabitants of the city

*Bialystok: memorial at Jewish cemetery site on Zabia Street to leaders and fighters of ghetto uprising (photo DHE, 1993)*

and approximately 200 of whom had survived the Bialystok ghetto. With the arrival of these Jews, the Zabia Street cemetery was quickly put in order, and the remains of the 3,500 ghetto victims were buried there. A wall was constructed around the cemetery, and several obelisks and a mausoleum were erected. Among the dead buried at the Zabia Street site were Aleksander Rajgrodzki; the chief editor of the daily *Dos Naje Leon*, Pejsach Kaplan; and the esteemed historian Samuel Herszberg.

Sadly, an anti-Semitic wave incited by the communist authorities in 1971 caused the cemetery to be destroyed and the monuments and obelisks to be torn down and blown up, replaced only by a small monument commemorating the Jews who perished in the ghetto. That and a fragment of the cemetery wall were all that remained of the cemetery until 1993, when a renovated obelisk, decorated with the Star of David, was dedicated in a public ceremony celebrated by the city's mayor and local dignitaries, Jewish visitors from all over the world, and Bialystok citizens.

*Cytron Bet ha Midrash*

When you've completed your visit to the memorial site at Zabia Street, retrace your route back to Aleja Pilsudskiego. You should be able to park easily near the bank, behind which a cobblestone street leads to 24-A Warynskiego Street (Polna Street before World War II). Here stands an attractive yellow building—now home to the Slendzinski Museum and Gallery as well as a tailor shop—bearing a plaque that describes its pre-World War II function as the Cytron Bet ha Midrash.

Built in 1936 during a period when few synagogues were constructed, the Ohel Szmuel ve Chawa Cytron synagogue was noteworthy for its richly ornamented ceilings, which were painted and made up in part of numerous elaborate combinations of various exotic woods. At a time when Jews were becoming increasingly integrated into Polish society and many had either ceased attending synagogue, were no longer religious, or had manifested anti-religious attitudes, people still came to this synagogue, built by Szmuel Cytron's four sons—Benjamin and Alex (who both later disappeared in Soviet camps) and Szymon and Jefim (who died in the United States)—to pray and appreciate its beauty. Its 150-light chandelier was designed by architect Israel Biskupicki and electrician Jakub Fiszer to hang in front of an ark with the Torah.

The Cytron synagogue's opening ceremony—which included a concert of liturgical music by the Chorshul choir (including both the Polish national anthem and the Jewish "Hatikwe") and performances by several well-known cantors—was attended by the mayor and the local commanding officers of the police and army.

If you proceed behind the synagogue (to 11/4 Aleja Pilsudskiego), you will see the three-story building that formerly served as David Druskin's Jewish Gymnasium. Among its graduates was Michael Flikier, a leader of Israel's Bialystok Jews. Today the building houses the Institute of Chemistry of Bialystok University.

## *Other Nearby and Noteworthy Places In and About Bialystok*

**Bema Street:** The site of a Jewish cholera cemetery that was in use from approximately 1840 to 1890. The cemetery was destroyed shortly after World War II.

**Jewish Hospital:** Built in the 1930s by the Society for the Protection of Health of the Jewish Population (TOZ), the hospital at 10 Fabryczna Street was one of the most modern hospitals in Bialystok. The building, which is still standing and still in use as a hospital, employs an interesting terraced architecture.

**Jewish Community Center and Library of Religious Books:** 2 Liniarskiego Street, next to the Russian Orthodox Church's regional administrative office. Dr. Gedali Rozenman, the chief rabbi of Bialystok, had an office here. The building has been renovated.

**Theater School:** 14 Sienkiewicza Street. Home to Jewish industrialist Zabludowski until 1939, this building was converted to a drama school after World War II. The building retains two of its original muraled ceilings, both of which look down upon stairways in what is still largely the original structure (see photo at left). You will also find a wrought iron Star of David on the northwest wall of the interior courtyard (see photo on next page).

**Pietrasze:** A forest at the northern edge of the city, entered from Wasilkowska Street (off Highway 18 towards Wasilkow). Reached by walking on a dirt road about one-half mile east of Highway 18, a small memorial park marks the forest location where German soldiers murdered (shot and buried in a mass grave) between 3,000 and 4,000 Jewish men, women and boys on

the 3rd and 11–13th of July 1941. Germans
also murdered approximately 100 Christians
here. A sign at the site provides details of
the tragedy (see photo on page 37).

**Grabowka:** At the eastern edge of Bialystok,
reached from Highway 66 towards
Bobrowniki, a monument commemorates
another forest location where a mass execu-
tion of Jews as well as Christians took place.

### Shorter Tours in Bialystok
### (One to Six Hours)

Realizing that your time in Bialystok may be limited, we offer six-
hour (by auto only), three-hour, and one-hour itineraries for your
visit. More detailed descriptions of stops along the route can be
found in the preceding sections.

## Six Hours (Including a meal.)

1) **Zabia Street** Site of the only ghetto cemetery in Poland. There
   is a monument commemorating ghetto fighters. Nearby, at 24-
   A Warynskiego St., is the restored building of the former
   Cytron Beth Midrash Synagogue. And next to this building (at
   Al. Pilsudskiego 11/4) is the three-story former David Druskin
   Gymnasium.

2) **10 Malmeda Street** Black marble plaque commemorating the
   murdered Icchok Malmed, one of the first Jewish fighters in
   the ghetto. Nearby, on Zamenhofa St., a plaque commemorates
   the Bialystok resident and creator of Esperanto, Ludwik
   Zamenhof.

3) **3 Piekna Street** The former Piaskower Beth Midrash synagogue, surrounded by what used to be the Jewish market,
   Rynek Sienny. Across from the synagogue, you can enjoy a
   meal at the Premiera restaurant.

4) **Kalinowskiego Street** City park on the site of a former Jewish cemetery. The cemetery's last *mazeva* can be found near the puppet theater.

5) **2 Liniarskiego Street** Former Jewish Community Center and Library of Religious Books. Next to the regional administrative office of the Orthodox Church. Dr. Gedali Rozenman, chief rabbi of Bialystok, had his office here.

6) **1 Suraska Street** Commemorative plaque in Polish and Hebrew: "To the Glorious Memory of 3,000 Jewish Martyrs burned alive in the Great Synagogue in Bialystok by Nazi murderers on June 24, 1941."

7) **Branicki Palace and Gardens** See page 50 for description.

8) **3 Branickiego Street** (near Branicki Palace). Site of the former Szmuel Beth Midrash synagogue.

9) **50 Warszawska Street** Iron sign on the street side wall of this apartment house has a Star of David. Two blocks west, at 15 Warszawska, is the former Jewish Maternity hospital.

10) **8 Warszawska Street** Gymnasium that numbered Ludwik Zamenhof among its pupils. There is a commemorative brass plaque on the building.

11) **10 Fabryczna Street** Former Jewish Hospital erected by the Society for the Protection of Health of the Jewish Population (TOZ) in the 1930s.

12) **Wschodnia Street** (easiest by auto, or by bus #3 or #9 from the city's center; about 5 km). 12-hectare, 7,000-tombstone Jewish cemetery with a monument to the Jewish victims of the 1906 pogrom. Rabbi Halpern's *ohel* is also here.

13) **Pietrasze Forest** (one-half mile east off Highway 18 going north to Wasilkow; reach by auto, or by bus #9 or #100; about 7.5 km from the city's center). Approximately 3,000 to 4,000 Jews were shot and murdered here on July 11–13, 1941. Some 100 Christians were also murdered and buried here.

**14) 79 Sienkiewicza Street** PCK Hospital, which was a Jewish gymnasium before the war. (Yitzhak Shamir, the former Prime Minister of Israel, was one of its graduates.)

*If your time is limited, I suggest the following for briefer tours by auto:*

## Three Hours: *(Without rushing.)*

Omit from above (the six-hour tour) items 4, 5, 10 and 11. You'll notice that several of the remaining sites are within easy walking distance of each other.

## One Hour

Visit only the following sites from the six-hour tour above:
1) Zabia Street; 2) 10 Malmeda Street; 6) 1 Suraska Street; 7) Branicki Palace and Gardens; 12) Wschodnia Street; 14) 79 Sienkiewicza Street.

Stick to the itinerary and keep moving, or you won't make it in an hour!

## OTHER TOWNS OF INTEREST IN THE
## BIALYSTOK REGION

Bialystok serves as a good starting point for trips to other parts of the region as well. Since you may want to go specifically to the area from which your ancestors hail, we do not offer any detailed itineraries for visits to the surrounding region. Instead, the information provided here is basic and brief, enough to help you determine your own itinerary. You can find more detailed information about all of the former Jewish communities in the Bialystok region by consulting *Synagogues and Jewish Communities in the Bialystok Region*, also written by Tomasz Wisniewski (Bialystok: Dom Wydawniczy David, 1992). Written primarily in Polish, it has many summary pages in English. It is available in Bialystok bookstores, or from the author (see page 136).

Simplified maps of most of these towns, showing the principal approaches and landmarks, appear at the beginning of each section.

### Bielsk Podlaski

*Population 26,826 (in 1993).*

*51 km south of Bialystok, via Highway 19.*

Although the first Jews appeared in this village in the 15th century, it was not until the next century that they formed a formal community. On May 30, 1487, King Kazimierz Jagiellonczyk made Jews the lease holders of customs

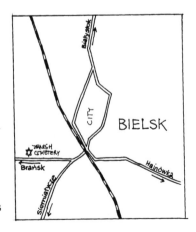

duty in Bielsk; in 1542 a formal community was created with a synagogue and a cemetery. However, in 1564 disagreements with the town's Christian inhabitants led to the Jews' expulsion, and they were not officially allowed to settle again until between 1802 and 1803. In 1807, a community was formed once again, this time under the jurisdiction of the Orla *kahal.* By 1878, as many

*Bielsk Podlaski: interior of the Great Synagogue, no longer standing, c. 1930 (collection TW)*

as 3,968 of Bielsk's 5,810 inhabitants were Jewish. Between World War I and World War II, about 2,500 Jews lived in Bielsk. The village's last rabbi was Moshe Aron Bendas.

Although none of Bielsk's four synagogues survived, you can still see the remains of the Jewish cemetery on the Bransk road, just behind the gas station. Outside the cemetery's entrance an obelisk has been erected to commemorate the "Polish citizens of Jewish nationality" shot by the Nazis. In addition, there are two tombstones erected by Jewish survivors. The rebuilt Jewish wash house (on Kazimierzowska Street) remains as evidence of Bielsk's Jewish past, and the 18th-century town hall (which now functions as a museum) is worth a visit. In the nearby village of Piliki, many Jews met their death.

In the early 19th century, townsman Roch Sikorski wrote the following about the Jews from Bielsk Podlaski:

Bielsk had privileges forbidding Jews to settle there, but like water seeping through hairline cracks, this nation came and spread widely. . . Not much can be said about Jews in our area, as they dress the same way as elsewhere, with perhaps the only difference being in their type of footwear. . . Jewish women, probably like elsewhere in Poland, wear headdresses set with pearls or other stones, while in the front of their dresses they had something with which to keep their hands warm. . . they also love lots of eiderdown and feather bed covers, and hang quilts above their beds. . . I kept away from them as much as I could since I had been prejudiced against them since childhood; however, I came to like one of them, by the name of Hersz, who traded in Bielsk and I even left small sums of money with him for my children, sure that I could trust him. . .

## Bocki

*Population 5,761 (in 1993).*

*68 km south of Bialystok, via Highway 19.*

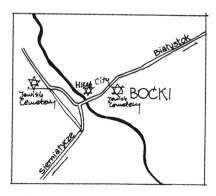

Bocki's Jewish community was formed in 1576, and the *Jewrejska Enciklopedia* reports that *mazevas* in the local cemetery date back to 1648 (though they are practically nonexistent today). In 1897, 1,409 of Bocki's 2,636 citizens were Jews; in the period just prior to World War II that number decreased to about 750. The village's last rabbis were Zelig Ruben Bengis and Joachen Mirski. The Nazis burned the 19th-century brick synagogue that contained a Torah from 1768 as well as silver collection boxes dating from 1740; they also torched a wooden house of prayer. The relics of Bocki's Jewish past that do remain include an early 19th-century brick-and-stone *mykva*—

which before World War II was used by both Jews and Christians—that is located by the river, next to the bridge. In addition, a wall fragment from the old Jewish cemetery (where only one *mazeva* survived) can be found next to a baroque church. The remains of the other

**Bocki:** *Jewish ritual bath, no longer in use (photo TW, 1986)*

cemetery—which comprised concrete tombstones without inscriptions—can be found in the southern part of town behind the river on the Jakubowskie road.

Jewish families who were named in a 1928 guidebook*
[*Ksiega Adresowa dla handlu, rzemiosl i przemyslu,* Warszawa: Bydgoszcz; 1928] include: "Medical doctor: Szlifenstein Josef Wolf; Hairdressers: Czesler Jonas, Kaczalski Chaim, Rubinstein Icchok; Grocers: Epstein Chaim, Farber Chaim, Kaplanski Szymon, Kosarska Chana, Kurlender Mozes, Zlotnik Moshe."

## Bransk

*Population 3,658 (in 1993).*

*57 km southwest of Bialystok, via Highway 681.*

The Jewish Community in Bransk was established in 1820. Before World War II this small town boasted as many as five houses of prayer as well as a Hasidim synagogue. It is interesting to note that 20 families of the local Hasidim represented different followers and belonged to five "dynasties": Kock, Aleksandrow, 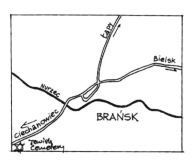 Kobryn, Radzyn and Slonim. Although no Jewish temples survived the war, Bransk is still worth visiting. So pious were the Jews in this town that when Rabbi Saul Denenberg departed from Bransk, a group prostrated themselves in front of his carriage and horses in an attempt to stop the rabbi. Denenberg's replacement, Rabbi Szmarie Margolis, earned the respect of both the Jewish and Christian communities. Another highly respected rabbi in the town and region was Jehuda Hakohen Szkop—the yeshiva he directed prior to World War I was attended by students from throughout the Russian empire.

Bransk's Jewish community was formed at the end of the 18th century, and by 1921, 2,165 of the town's 3,739 inhabitants were Jews. Bransk's last rabbi was Icchok Cukierman (Zukerman).

---

* Referred to hereafter simply as "the 1928 guide."

**Bransk:** *Jewish cemetery (photo TW, 1986)*

Today's only reminder of Bransk's Jewish past is its cemetery, which contains a common grave for the 68 Jews and two Poles shot here on November 16, 1942. (The Bransk Town Council plans to put a new granite plaque in place listing the victims of this slaughter.) To reach the cemetery—which is tended by the Society of Friends of Bransk— drive across town toward Ciechanowiec, passing the bridge over the Nurzec and the first crossroad before turning left in the direction of Brzeznice. You will see a sign for the cemetery just after you make the turn. Recently, a wall was begun to enclose the cemetery; in fact, the Bransk *kirkut* (cemetery) is one of the few Polish cemeteries that continues to grow (as a rule, they shrink and lose their "stone" substance).

Today the Brzeznice cemetery contains more than 200 *mazevas*, many of them cleaned and painted, all of them numbered. Local historian and researcher Zbigniew Romaniuk (Bransk, Sienkiewicza 24, tel. 0834726) registers and translates the *mazevas*, which he recovers (together with a group of friends) from sidewalks, curbs, and town roads, where they have been built into the pavement. Zbigniew—a young gentile who has served as the town's vice-mayor—has a collection of Bransk judaics as well as the computerized register of the 2,300 Jews who lived in Bransk

**Bransk:** *Hinda Sasin in Jewish cemetery, 1926; tombstone no longer there (photographer unkown, courtesy Zbigniew Romanivk*

from the mid-19th century through 1939. The Town Hall offices are at 8 Rynek, telephone 142.

The village of Bransk—and Zbigniew Romaniuk's work in restoring its Jewish monuments—were featured in Marian Marzynski's three-hour PBS film documentary "Frontline: Shtetl." Bransk is also the subject of Eva Hoffman's book *Shtetl: The Life and Death of a Small Town and the World of Polish Jews* (Boston: Houghton Mifflin Company, 1997).

The following are some of the deciphered *mazeva* inscriptions, with the date of death:

1845 — Chaja Roza, daughter of Morejnu Jakow
1846 — Abraham Cvi, son of Marejn Dawid Hakohen
1847 — Mordechaj, son of Gedali
1868 — Efroim, son of Abraham
1873 — Fejga Roza, daughter of Jakow
1875 — Rachel, daughter of Nizan
1879 — Chaja, daughter of David
1880 — Basza, daughter of Cvi
1881 — Nechama, daughter of Josif
1888 — Bacalal, son of Naftali
1889 — Dow Arie, son of Moshe
1890 — Rafira, daughter of Josif
1891 — Terna, daughter of Pesach
1892 — Frida, daughter of Moshe
1892 — Chai Pasza, daughter of Dowa
1893 — Josif, son of Mordechaj
1894 — Riwka, daughter of Israel
1913 — Meir Jehuda, son of Jakow
1913 — Sara Riwka, daughter of Zelman Jakow
1913 — Pasza Miriam, daughter of Zelig Icchok
1914 — Bejla, daughter of Dowa
1915 — Rachel, daughter of Icchok
1915 — Moshe Eliau, son of Abraham Halewi
1916 — Chai Riwka, daughter of Moshe, wife of Moshe Juda
1917 — Eliezer, son of Jakow Arie
1918 — Cvi, son of Szmul Jehuda
1920 — Basza Sima, daughter of Arie
1921 — Nachum, son of Moshe Elizer
1921 — Moshe Elchanan, son of Dowa
1922 — Chaja Riwka Prybut, daughter of Arie Lejba

1922 — Chaja Riwka, daughter of Moshe
1922 — Menachem Mendel, son of Eliezer
1925 — Rachela, daughter of Jakow ha-Kohen
1927 — Jenta, daughter of Fiszel
1928 — Elka, daughter of Zelig Dawid, wife of Alter Wilk
1932 — Hania, daughter of Icchak, wife of Abraham Winer
1934 — Eliau Natan, son of Mordechaj Arie Glazar
1938 — Dawid Biber
1941 — Joszua Elchanan, son of Szloma, and Leja Ruchama,
       daughter of Benjamin
1941 — Eliau Gerszon, son of Cvi Icchak

## Choroszcz

*Population 5,223 (in 1993).*

*9 km east of Bialystok, via Highway 18.*

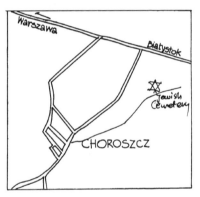

Until World War II,
Choroszcz—known primarily
for its psychiatric hospital and
the small baroque palace that
served as hetman Jan Klemens
Branicki's summer residence—
was a town of four religions:
Jewish, Catholic, Orthodox and
Protestant.

The town's Jewish commu-
nity dates from 1566, and just
prior to World War II,
Choroszcz counted 800 Jews among its residents. Lejb Rywkind
was the town's last rabbi before later becoming a member of the
German-created *Judenrat*. During the war, Choroszcz's Jews were
first moved to a camp in Bialystok's *Nowe Miasto* (New Town) and
then later transferred to Treblinka, where they were murdered.

Neither the town's main wooden synagogue (which was on
the market square) nor the old cemetery (in the center of the village, by the Russian Orthodox church) remain today. Only one
Jewish cemetery, with 259 *mazevas*, remains (at the edge of the forest along the road from town to Lyski). The local people who
carefully tend this cemetery recently removed some of the bushes
and fenced in and marked the area.

The following are inscriptions, with date of death, from some of the *mazevas*:

1894 — Daniel, son of Samuel
1880 — Aron Bamach Kojzesz
1834 — Rabbi Zintman, strangled
1904 — Mejer Jechijel Meibel
1866 — Moshe Rubin Chackiel Skotalnik
        Masza, de domo Arie Judel
1937 — Sara Gitel Aleksander
        Chaja Rachel, rabbi's wife
1930 — Fruma, daughter of Rejzel
1908 — Sara, daughter of Arie Lejb

## Dabrowa Bialostocka

*Population 6,571 (in 1993).*

*73 km north of Bialystok; 24 km north of Sokolka.*

The Jewish community here was established toward the end of the 18th century, and throughout the 19th century Dabrowa Bialostocka remained a truly Jewish town in which the percentage of Jewish inhabitants varied from 45 to 85 percent. In 1880 the town numbered 1,132 Jews, 264 Catholics, 29 Muslims, and 13 Russian Orthodox among its inhabitants. In the mid-1930s, approximately 1,550 of the town's 3,550 residents were Jews. In 1938 the last of Dabrowa's anti-Semitic riots took place. Moshe Gerszon Mowszowicz was rabbi until 1932, when he was followed by Chaim Kac.

Prior to World War II, Dabrowa was home to several functioning synagogues and two cemeteries. Of these, only the cemetery on Sztabinska Street (in the western part of town) remains. Picturesquely situated atop a hill, the cemetery has retained about 70 *mazevas*, several of them noteworthy for their unusually clear Hebrew inscriptions. In 1995 a fence was built around the cemetery with an iron gate at the entrance. A stone monument memor-

**Dabrowa:** *stone monument memorial in Jewish cemetery (photo TW, 1995)*

ial was also installed and dedicated in a ceremony in June 1995 (see photo).

Also of interest in Dabrowa is an old Jewish *mykva* building which is now being used as a mill.

Jewish families named in the 1928 guide include: "Tailors: Borenstein Aron, Goldstein Tanchum, Irolski Abram, Kaplan Moshe, Lewin Judel, Orlanski Chaim, Szulak Szymon."

To learn more about Dabrowa's history, contact local poet, writer, and historian Mikolaj Samojlik at 2 Sloneczna Street (telephone, 121-275), or Jan Zarzecki, who lives near the Jewish cemetery on Sztabinska Street. Mr. Zarzecki also has a key to the cemetery entrance gate.

## Drohiczyn

*Population 2,186 (in 1993).*

*114 km south of Bialystok; 15 km east of Siemiatycze.*

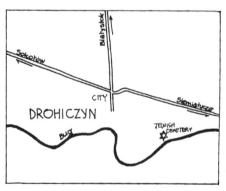

Drohiczyn is well worth seeing on any tour, not only for its small Jewish forest cemetery but for the town itself, as it is the oldest in the region. In the 12th and 13th centuries the town was the capital of a Russian duchy before acquiring its "city" status and privileges in 1408.

Located on the high banks of the Bug River, in the 18th century Drohiczyn became a river harbor. Now the seat of a Catholic bishop, the town has three Catholic church complexes dating from the 16th century. It also contains an 18th-century Russian Orthodox church. Rising above the city is Castle Mountain, where visitors can view the ruins of a medieval castle or simply admire the winding Bug River below. All of these features combine to make Drohiczyn an attractive summer destination for painters, photographers, archaeologists, and film-makers.

*Drohiczyn: part of the Jewish market, c. World War I; Catholic church in background (photo Herder Institute, Marburg)*

Although Jews first appeared in Drohiczyn at the end of the 13th century, a true Jewish community did not form until the 18th century. By 1931, Drohiczyn's Jewish residents numbered 711. The last rabbis were Mordechaj Izaak Tirnawski and Aron Bystryn.

Today a small cemetery on the banks of the Bug River (about 1,800 meters east of the city) contains the only evidence of the Jewish presence in this town's thousand-year history. The cemetery is difficult to find and the area overgrown with trees. Even if you have a detailed map, you'd be best off asking for assistance. Your persistence will be rewarded, as many *mazevas* remain. The following are included among the inscriptions that have been deciphered, with date of death:

1889 — Krejzel, daughter of Abraham
1887 — Jakuab, son of Dow Ber
1891 — Jehuda Lejb, son of Matan Hakohen
1918 — Jehuda, son of Mordechaj
1900 — Liba Frejda, daughter of Zundel
1910 — Moshe, son of Joel
1876 — Sara, daughter of Jakub

*Drohiczyn: Jews welcome papal nuncio, c. 1930 (photo Society of Friends of Drohiczyn)*

1898 — Chaja, daughter of Benjamin
1910 — Szloma Zelig, son of Moshe Icchok
1898 — Moshe Icchok, son of Naftali Herszel
1919 — Fejga Rywka, daughter of Josef
1912 — Fejga Debiora, daughter of Meir Zew Ha Lewi
1922 — Jehuda Lejb, son of Abraham Ha Lewi
1927 — Jakow, son of Moshe Ukrainczyk from Sokolow

For more information about Drohiczyn, contact Urszula Tomasik, the director of the local cultural center and the Regional Museum on Kraszewskiego Street.

## Grodek

*Population 6,957 (in 1993).*

*37 km east of Bialystok, via Highway 66.*

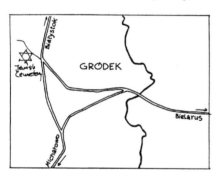

The charming town of Grodek is located on the so called "Eastern wall" of Poland. Almost entirely inhabited by Belarussian Orthodox church members today, little remains of Grodek's once large Jewish community. The first Jews came to Grodek in 1614 and the Jewish community grew rapidly. At the end of the 19th century (1897 census), 78 percent of the town's 2,513 citizens were Jewish. None of the town's five synagogues remain standing today, and only a few relics of the Jewish cemetery can be found in the northwest part of the town, near a Christian cemetery. These include several concrete gravestones as well as the *mazevas* built into Grodek's roads and sidewalks. The town's last rabbis were Nisan Brojde and Abram Zelig Syjon.

Jewish families named in the 1928 guide: "Mills: Goldstein family, Jelin Symcha, Rudy Ruwen, Kaplan Szymon; Textile factory: Amdurski Fajwel, Lunski Abram, Pruzanski & Repelski. Watchmaker: Fajnzylberg Moshe."

Near Grodek, in the village of Walily, lives Leon Tarasewicz, the region's best known painter. His paintings have been shown in galleries around the world. His telephone is 180-508.

## Jalowka

*Population 650 (in 1993).*

*61 km east of Bialystok, close to the Belarussian border.*

The first Jews arrived in Jalowka in 1690 and the Jewish community was established in 1708. The census of 1878 counted 743 Jews—most of whom were coppersmiths and carpenters—among the town's 1,311 residents. Approximately 100 Jewish families lived here just before the outbreak of World War II. In addition, prior to the war, Jalowka was known as a summer holiday retreat, and

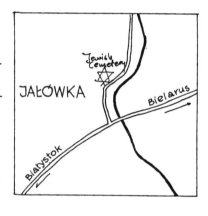

Jews from Bialystok and other cities stayed in the town's many cottages on weekends and holidays. The town's last rabbi was Icchok "Icek" Podorowski.

Of the Jews from Jalowka, contemporary Belarussian author Alex Barski wrote in a local Belarussian newspaper:

They were the poorest group among Jews in the period between the two world wars. . . They used to go from one village to another and buy all kinds of old clothes. In

*Jalowka: Jewish ritual bath, now a warehouse (photo TW, 1988)*

return they gave various small items: needles, thimbles, matches, spoons. There was one Jew who bought only empty bottles, which he broke immediately and threw into his wagon. Probably that was the condition in which the glass factory bought them. . .

The same author blamed postwar inhabitants of Jalowka and the surrounding area for destroying the remains of the Jewish cemetery for their own use:

The slabs could be used as grindstones as they were rounded at the top. All one had to do was round the bottom part and a grindstone for sharpening knives was ready. And such tools started appearing in local villages. After a while it turned out that the Jewish graves ceased to exist. . .

On the Kondratki road (200 meters north of Jalowka) you will come across the remains of a Jewish cemetery with several *mazevas*. Although nothing is left of the old cemetery in the town center, a large Jewish *mykva* remains on the Jalowka River.

Jewish families named in the 1928 guide: "Bakers: Kagan Fajwel and Ruben, Satyr Ruben. Leather workers: Goldberg Owadia, Goldshmidt Moshe. Store with iron: Berenstein Judel, Pelic Judel, Rozowski Moshe."

### Janow Sokolski

*Population 4,920 (in 1993).*

*49 km north of Bialystok.*

Jews began to settle in Janow as early as the 17th century, and by 1719 the bishop of Vilno, Konstanty Brzostowski, had granted them permission to build a synagogue (which was constructed in 1740). The town's census in 1775 counted 214 Christian residents and 221 Jews. In 1897, 1,797 (or 78 percent) of the town's 2,296 residents were Jewish. Just prior to World War II, approximately 1,100 Jews lived in this small, poor town known for its hotel, which was owned by the Jew Chmiel Rudawski. The last rabbis of Janow were Nisan Perelsztejn, Jehoszua Kralusz, and Zalman Kosowski. The town's wooden synagogue, which prior to World War II was renovated and maintained by the Polish State Office for Historical Buildings, was burned and destroyed by the Nazis.

A Jewish cemetery remains in the northern part of Janow (on the way to Kuplisk and Kamienica). The cemetery—which is not fenced in in any way—contains about 200 *mazevas* as well as the remains of a brick gate.

Jewish families named in the 1928 guide: "Medicine doctors and pharmacy: Chassin Ruben, Shapiro Maria, Goldstein Gershon. Butchers: Bobrowicz Chaim, Nowokolski Mendel."

## Jasionowka

*Population 3,408 (in 1993).*

*41 km north of Bialystok.*

The Jewish settlement dates from the beginning of the 16th century. The influx of Jews a century later was connected with the appearance of the Tartars who developed leather manufacturing handled by Jewish merchants. In 1799, the town's population was 683 and 346 were Jews. Two synagogues (one brick) were partly destroyed by the Germans and pulled down after the war. The last rabbi of Jasionowka was Tanchum Gerszon Bilicki.

A Jewish cemetery (started at the end of 19th century) remains between the roads north to Slomianki and northeast to Korycin. There are more than 400 *mazevas* left. The town's oldest Jewish cemetery (founded in the 18th century) is in the center of the village. A few tombs still survive.

The inscriptions, with date of death, on some of the *mazevas* in the 19th-century cemetery :

1843 — Szlomo son Eliezer
1935 — Josif son of Abram Moshe Wojtechowski
1838 — Tewie Szlomo Moshe son of Chawes
1918 — Fruma Daicz daughter of Szmuel
1866 — Hilach daugher of Mejer Dawid Segal
1836 — Szmuel Gitlin or Gutlin

Some Jewish residents who are mentioned in records dating from the end of the 19th century are: Mowsza Lejb Glogowski, Kalman Chodowski, Lejb Grochman, Aron Riwlin, Mowszo Jaskowski, Wolf Lewin, Lejba Suchowolski, Lejb Korek, Zelman Gelborn, Icko Brzezinski, Chackiel Kronenberg, Abram and Moszko Suraski.

*Jasionowka: general view, 1916; in background, roofs of two synagogues, no longer standing (photographer unknown; collection TW)*

## Kleszczele

*Population 1,678 (in 1993).*

*77 km south of Bialystok.*

In the 16th century Izaac Brodawka from Brzesc (now "Brest" in Belarus) received a royal privilege to build a brewery in Kleszczele. From then until 1688 there existed a small Jewish community within the town. This community reappeared at the beginning of the 19th century, and by 1897, 710 of the town's 2,013 residents were Jews. In 1931, 645 of the town's 2,053 residents were Jews.

All that remains today of Kleszczele's Jewish past are the almost nonexistent ruins of the Jewish cemetery (south on the Czeremcha road about 1,500 meters, just beyond a bakery and adjacent to the forest). Only several *mazevas* survive. There is also a recently-placed, small memorial tomb.

If you want more information about Kleszczele, you must be sure to visit Maria Klimowicz while you're in town. The publisher of a local paper and director of the local cultural center, Klimowicz has been collecting relics of the town's past, including its Jewish history. In addition, the State Archive in Bialystok (in the materials of the Elder Notary of Grodno) contains some of the names of Jewish inhabitants of Kleszczele. (The date shown is the date recorded by the Notary):

1884 — Kalman Wolfowicz Bezdiecki
1884 — Mowszo Mordko Gwin
1884 — Moshe Judel Szmul
1885 — Kalman Wolf Bezdiecki
1885 — Lejman Waniewska, Herszko Berko Melamed Blumenfeld
1885 — Aron Gersz Zajbman
1893 — Gerszko Fajwel Kleszczalski, Szmuel Nat Minc
1894 — Wolf Josef Pinkas Poloniecki, Noski Jos Krinkier
1900 — Abram Lejb Kielmanowicz Linde
1900 — Micha Jankiel Morianski, Lejbko Kalman Lilede
1903 — Judes Ester Fajwel Wajnsztajn, Mowszo Fiszel Haskiel,
       Berko Lejb Domaracki
1904 — Mowszo Mordko Pin
1904 — Mowszo Mardko Gwin
1908 — Abram Lejba Kalman Linder Lindus Ertel Leja David
       Wysocki

# Knyszyn

*Population 2,937 (in 1993).*

*27 km northwest of Bialystok, via Highway 669.*

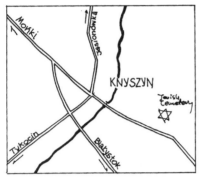

In Knyszyn you have a town with more than 500 years of history. Once the residence of Polish kings (in the 16th and 17th centuries), it was here in 1572 that the last king of the Jagiellonian dynasty, Sigismundus Augustus, met his end. His memorial tomb was opened in 1997. Today, however, there is little to suggest to visitors Knyszyn's former importance, except perhaps the 200-year-old wooden granary that sits next to a frequently rebuilt church on Koscielna Street. On the same street (at No. 6), you will find Cecylia Plasecka, a true encyclopedia of the town. This stylish elderly lady, who is always quick with a smile and a friendly word, has collected town relics for many years and maintains a private archive detailing the lives of Knyszyn's Jews.

As early as the 16th century, Jews were already living near the royal residence in Knyszyn. And although Knyszyn townsmen obtained the privilege *de non tolerandis judaeis* (forbidding Jews to settle in the town) in the middle of the 17th century, Jews continued to reside here. By the outbreak of World War II, approximately 1,400 of the town's 4,000 inhabitants were Jews. Professor Moshe Miszkinski, the son of Knyszyn's last rabbi, now lives in Israel where he is a well-known historian. Another Knyszyn-born Jew, Sol Solasz, is now the president of the Bialystoker Center in New

**Knyszyn:** *tombstones in the Jewish cemetery (photo TW, 1986)*

York City (228 East Broadway, New York, NY 10002, tel. 212/475-7755). (The Center is a home for senior citizens, many of whom are former residents of Bialystok. The Center also has published a number of books and magazines with information about Bialystok and its Jewish families. It is supported by a membership who live around the world.)

Although neither of Knyszyn's two synagogues has survived, the town is home to one of the most unusually located Jewish cemeteries in Europe. To visit this cemetery, proceed south from the market square in the direction of Chraboly. After you cross the bridge over the Jaskrzanka River, you will pass the first intersection of field roads before a densely forested area comes into view on your left. This is the site of the Jewish cemetery; however, to reach it, you must follow the path leading to the left. When you reach your destination, the first thing you'll see will be several Jewish tombstones from the so-called "new Jewish cemetery," which opened around 1930. Much more interesting, however, is the well-preserved older cemetery, which was established in the second half of the 18th century on the town's abandoned royal ponds and built by Piotr Chwalczewski, who served as Knyszyn's *starosta* (administrator) from 1553 to 1564. Today the cemetery is maintained by, among others, scouts from the local schools.

Originally numbering 19, only seven of the royal ponds still remained by 1939. Today these ponds provide the only observable reminders of the former royal residence. During King Sigismundus Augustus's reign, the ponds' dams served as a refuge for such game as deer and rabbits (with hunting prohibited). However, by 1750, the ponds had fallen into neglect and were not bringing in any profit and thus were sold by the city to the Jewish community, which had already established a cemetery in the area. Since they were overgrown and littered with potholes by the time of the German occupation, the effort of removing large stones from this labyrinthine cemetery was simply too costly and labor-intensive for the Nazis to carry out; thus, the cemetery escaped destruction.

The dams function as cemetery paths, defining the overall space. The oldest *mazevas* are concentrated in the western portion of the cemetery, and many are worth examining. Take, for example, the richly ornamented stone with the sophisticated relief drawing of a lion holding religious books in its paws. Or the elab-

orate epitaphs that characterize so many of these *mazevas*. Here is
one example:

*...The joy of our heart died*
*the fiddle plays a funeral tune*
*our misfortune is as large as the sea* ...
*angels cry* ... *the glory of our community lost its horns* ...
*the Tzadik* ... *his mouth was full of precious stones*
*among brothers of work, he spread the faith* ...

The following names, with dates of death, are among those
deciphered and translated from the approximately 700 *mazevas* in
the Jewish cemetery in Knyszyn (the fourth-largest collection after
Bialystok, Krynki, and Sokolka):

1807 — Gimpel Zew Mordechaj
1811 — Rabbi Cwi Eliezer Litman
1815 — Bejla, daughter of Iszaj Hakohen
1819 — Cywia Zela, daughter of Rabbi Jehoszua
1830 — Zew Wolf, son of Marie Kac
1831 — Cwi Hirsz, son of Israel
1831 — Arie Lew Wolf Kac
1839 — Tomb of Leja Rozenberg, daughter of Mordechaj
1863 — Icchok, son of Gaon Jezekiel Haifec, author of "New
         Roads"
1863 — Etel, daughter of Sachar Goniadski
1866 — Abraham, son of Szlomo Ajzyk Trekenberg
1880 — Sarah, daughter of Icchok Goniadski
1882 — Menachem Mendel, son of Jakub Suraski
1887 — Rabin Sincha, son of Rabbi Abraham
1895 — Naftali Herc Hakohen Szlomo
1911 — Mejer Aronson, son of Jakow Bursztyn
1913 — Kol Bochin, son of Arie
1916 — Jezekiel David Kanacinski (or "Karacianski")
1922 — Jezekiel David Brajser Kanacinski
1924 — Golda, daughter of Saul Kaplan
1925 — Rabin Arje, son of Efroim Wajnsztajn
1927 — Sijon Icchok Cwi Zuskowicz
1928 — Szlomo Mordechaj, son of Zwi Hacochen
1928 — Elijahu Arie, son of Icchok Ajzyk
1928 — Ester Epsztejn

1928 — Mariasza, daughter of Abram Badszymczuski
1928 — Jakow Lopacinski
1930 — Abraham Symcha Loszowki
1930 — Szlomo Michal, son of David Sztejn
1930 — Moshe Icchok, son of Giesel Orsikowski
1931 — Fejga Zapasner, daughter of Kopel
1931 — Hilel, son of Szewach Pitkowski
1931 — Henia Chenia Leja, wife of famous Rabbi Tanchum
     Grynszpan, daughter of Rabbi Beniamin Klejnerman
1932 — Mejer, son of Abraham Grynszpan
1932 — Chana, daughter of Jekutiel Hkohen Szpitalnik
No date — Sarah Pesze, daughter of Aron Icchok Orlanski
1935 — Aron, son of Mordechaj Jasionowski
1936 — Jehudit Krywlanski, daughter of Josef
1936 — Lipa, son of Symcha Slodownik
1936 — Rachel, daughter of Szmuel, wife of David Icchok Kulik
1937 — Jehoszua, son of Arie Lipszyc
No date — Leja, wife of Rabbi Cohen Oszenbach
No date — Arie (?) Rozenblum
No date — Rabbi Zew Wolf, son of Cwi Karp Karf
1941 (Tomb erected in 1970) — Sima Brzezinska, Malka Czeslar,
     Perla Brzezinska

Before Knyszyn's town hall was renovated the building contained a plaque commemorating those who had been murdered by the Nazis during the November 2, 1942, evacuation when 72 Jews were shot on the spot. However, the text of the plaque did not indicate that the murdered were Jewish. Plans are under way now to revise the wording and replace the plaque in the new museum of Knyszyn.

If you are interested, in the local archives in Knyszyn you can find records concerning Jews from Knyszyn (births, deaths, and marriage certificates).

## Korycin

*Population 900 (in 1993).*

*39 km north of Bialystok, via Highway 19.*

Established in the mid-17th century, Korycin's Jewish community became such that in 1722 a historian noted that "the town was inhabited only by Jews." While this may have been an exaggeration, Jews did make up a significant segment of the population. In 1897, 411 of the town's 683 residents were Jews, and just prior to World War II, approximately 350 Jewish citizens lived in Korycin. Chaim Mojzson was the town's last rabbi.

What little of the town's Jewish cemetery that survived the Holocaust can be found in the southern portion of the village by the Krukowszczyzna road. The Nazis used the cemetery's stone wall and *mazevas* to build a road between Korycin and Jasionowika, and the cemetery itself was plowed. Still, several *mazevas* remain at the former site.

Prior to World War II, Korycin had one small hotel, which was owned by a man named Brudny (dirty). The doctor's name was Polak, and the mayor's Szwed (Swede). Hence the saying originated that only in Korycin is there one dirty (Brudny) hotel, one Polak who is Jewish, and one Mayor who is a Swede!

## Kry̲nki

*Population 4,056 (in 1993).*

*47 km east of Bialystok, via Highway 676.*

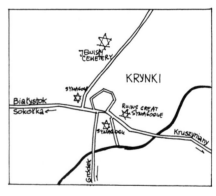

Jews settled in Krynki in the middle of the 17th century, and in 1639 received the privilege from King Wladislaw to buy land and build houses there. In 1662 they received permission to erect a synagogue and a washhouse as well as found a Jewish cemetery. Larger even than the Bialystok community, 1,285 Jews inhabited the town and surrounding area by 1765, representing the second-largest community in the kahal (after the regional community in Grodno).

In the 18th and 19th centuries, Krynki was the most orthodox and religious Jewish community in the Bialystok region. (The National Library in Jerusalem contains a religious book titled *Szaagad Arie, The Lion's Roar*. The book was printed in Bialystok in 1805 by Aharon A' Lewi Hurwic and written by Arie Lejb, Krynki's rabbi. He was the son of rabbi Bendit from Zabludow,

grandson of rabbi Chaim Klonimus Katz, great-grandson of a
Cracow rabbi and the son-in-law of a rabbi from Hamburg. The
author signed his work "temporarily in Krynki," meaning that he
perceived Palestine as his future permanent residence, a practice
common among rabbis from Central and Eastern Europe.)
In 1876, Jews made up an estimated 85 percent of the town's
3,336 residents. During the Holocaust the Germans created a ghetto in Krynki. When the Nazis decided to liquidate it, the Jews of
Krynki actively opposed them, killing several of the German murderers.

In 1929, the town's vice mayor was the Jew David Gotlib. The
last rabbi to serve Krynki was Josif Hezekiel Miszkowski, who
now lives in Israel where he is the leader of one of the more
orthodox religious factions.

Although Krynki is now only a small village, prior to World
War I it was a rapidly developing town with scores of small factories and workshops. Located by the border, it now feels small and
sleepy, as if lost in memories of its past. Krynki does, however,
still retain some links to its history, and the visible remains of
Krynki's Jewish ancestry are suprisingly many.

On the western side of the market square (at Gorna Street)
stands the 19th-century "Kaukaski" Beth Midrash brick synagogue, which now functions as a movie theater. On Grochowa
Street, at the corner of Czysta, stands a brick building that housed
another former synagogue (Jentes Beth Midrash), this one
Hasidim. The building is now a warehouse.

Continuing through the village of Krynki, you will come
across the ruins of the Great Synagogue at Garbarska Street.
Erected in 1756, the Great Synagogue was enormous for its time
(twice as large as both the town's Catholic church and Orthodox
church). Inadequate preservation and the fear that its granite
walls would collapse thwarted plans to rebuild and convert the
temple into a movie theater or cultural center.

Krynki is also home to a large Jewish cemetery. In fact with
more than 3,000 *mazevas*, it may well be the largest shtetl Jewish
cemetery in Poland. The oldest identified *mazevas* are from the
middle of the 18th century. One curiosity is a stone wall with
numbers inscribed identifying the rows of the buried. This was
done by members of Hewre Kadisha Society who have maintained the cemetery. On one of the *mazevas*, we were able to deci-

## Some Views of Krynki Synagogues

*Ruins of great synagogue, after World War II (photo collection TW)*

*Interior of great synagogue, before World War II (photo courtesy of Yivo Institute for Jewish Research, New York)*

*Synagogue "Kaukaski," used as cinema after World War II, now restored (photo TW)*

*Chassidic synagogue (photo TW, 1987)*

pher the following inscription fragment: "Avoid nationalism unti the end of your days."

The following names, with date of death, are among those that can be deciphered at the cemetery:

1758 — Chaim, son of Beniamin
1799 — Rachel, daughter of Lejb Szenapa
1834 — Szewach, daughter of Szebsel

1836 — Beniamin, son of Abraham
1845 — Szmuelson, son of Icchok Szynapet
1878 — Sarah Rajna, daughter of Josif
1879 — Israel Iser, son of Hilel
1901 — Rabbi Jehoszua, son of Arie
1911 — Szlomo, son of Abraham Ab Aw (?)
1912 — Masza, daughter of Eliezer Moshe Poczebucki
1913 — Pesia Raszkies Knyszynska, daughter of Szmuel
1917 — Szmuel Meir, son of Becalel Elkany
1918 — Chaja Liba Frydman, daughter of rabbi Elijahu
1918 — Neska Grossman, daughter of rabbi Szmuel
1918 — Szprynca, daughter of rabbi Israel Musaf
1920 — Cypa, daughter of Jehoszua Icchok Skowronek
1921/22 — Awigail, daughter of rabbi Mejer Zapsztejn vel Zalkin
1921 — Miret Mecadok, daughter of Josef Lewit
1928 — Nachum Anszyl, son of Mordche Knyszynski
1932 — Manes Dwukamienski, son of Szmuel vel Sofer
1933 — Jakow Iser, son of Efroim Kugel
1934 — Manes Zew Icchok, son of Jakow Szuliatski
1934 — Jechuda Nachum, son of Israel Arie Garber
1934 — Beniamin, son of Elijahu Chawes Laziebnik
1936 — Cadyk, son of Abraham Jatowszyk

On your way back from Krynki, you might consider taking a
short detour to visit the village of Grzybowszczyzna. It is an
attractive village of old wooden houses. It was also here in the
1930s that the Russian Orthodox church of St. John the Baptist
was erected as a center for followers of the small religious sect of
the Prophet Eliasz Klimowicz, who announced the coming of the
end of the world. The sect has followers even today.

## Kuznica

*Population 5,079 (in 1993).*

*58 km northeast of Bialystok, via Highway 18.*

The Jewish community in Kuznica dates from 1623, and by 1897 it
included 780 Jews, or 58 percent of the village's 1,346 residents.
By 1931, that number had decreased to 556 (out of 1,426 inhabitants). From 1894 until World War II, Ajzyk Lejb Stolar was the
town's rabbi. The brick synagogue, which was architecturally the
most interesting building in the town, did not survive the

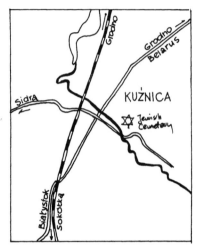

Holocaust. Several *mazevas* remain in Kuznica's Jewish cemetery, which is located close to Podlipska Street on a hill above the Zwegra River. The town has plans to fence in the cemetery and place a memorial plaque at the entrance.

Jewish families named in the 1928 guide: "Blacksmiths: Kotlar Moshe, Lipshic Mendel, Nowodzielski Abram; grocery stores: Adin Ruben, Epstein & Fajnsod, Frydlanski Abram, Halpern Gershon, Kryglanski Moshe, Lipcer Efroim, Wilenski Chaim, Zelwianska Inda."

*Kuznica: synagogue built at end of 18th century, c. 1930; no longer standing (photo Szymon Zajczyk(?), courtesy Institute of Art PAN, Warsaw)*

## Lapy

*Population 17,471 (in 1993).*

*27 km southwest of Bialystok, via Highway 682.*

The town of Lapy was created in 1925 when six villages with "Lapy" in their names were combined. The town's development paralleled that of the major railroad station and train workshops located there. In approximately 1880, a Jewish community was formed and a house of prayer erected in Lapy. In about 1900 a large synagogue was built. The town's Jewish population increased significantly with the influx of Jews from nearby Suraz, when that town burned in 1916. According to the 1921 census, 623 of the town's 3,495 inhabitants were Jews. Lapy's last rabbi was Lejb Blousztejn. Nazis burned the town's wooden synagogue, and the community did not have its own cemetery. (Lapy Jews were initially buried in the Suraz cemetery and then after World War I at cemeteries in Bialystok and Sokoly.) All that remains today of Lapy's Jewish heritage is a brick building that contained a *mykva* that was available to all of the town's inhabitants. It is now a furniture store and is at 11 Listopada Street, close to the railway station.

Jewish families named in the 1928 guide: "Kagan Icko, Wajner Moshe, Szenfeld Berko, Fales Mendel, Lachower Icko, Grynberg Hirsz, Rozen Samuel, Zolty Judel, Segalowicz Lipa."

## Michalowo

*Population 8,827 (in 1993).*

*38 km east of Bialystok and 10 km south of Grodek.*

Jews settled in this industrial town at the beginning of the 19th century, and by 1921, 887 of the town's 2,176 inhabitants were Jews. The town also included a fairly large German population, and marriages between Jews and Germans were common prior to World War II. Michalowo's last rabbi was Saul Margolis.

In days gone by Michalowo's house of prayer was accessible via a brick stairway; today, however, the temple is gone and the steps lead nowhere. You will find the remains of the Jewish cemetery off the Zednia road, approximately 1.5 kilometers from town on the road leading west to Bialystok. When you reach the sign for Majdan, turn right and venture into the forest. Unfortunately, the road stops before it reaches the cemetery, which is located on a high forest slope where *mazevas* were placed among the pines. With no fence to identify the cemetery, its boundaries are unclear, and even the people of Michalowo are uncertain of its precise location. However, approximately 50 *mazevas* remain as evidence of a true Jewish cemetery on the edge of the Knyszyn Forest.

Jewish families named in the 1928 guide: "Pharmacy: Gerszuni Fajwel; Mills: Frydman Moshe, Kaplan Chaim, Nejman Aharon. Textile factories: Cytron Lipa, Frajmark Walach, Laznik & Goldfarb."

For more information about Michalowo's Jewish residents, you can contact local historian Dr. Leszek Nos at 2 Szkolna Street.

## Mielnik

*Population 3,150 (in 1993).*

*122 km south of Bialystok and 23 km southeast of Siemiatycze.*

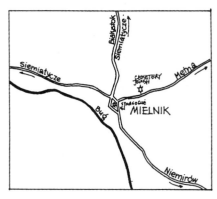

Picturesquely located on the Bug River, Mielnik is one of the oldest towns in the region. Dating from the 10th or 11th century, it finally became a town in 1440. Today all that remains of its former glory are the ruins of the 15th-century church and a castle that was destroyed by the Tartars in 1241. In addition, the ruins of a 16th-century castle can be found in the hills above the town, and the chalk pit on the outskirts of town is one of the largest in Europe.

Jews were present in Mielnik as early at 1533 and probably formed their first community there around 1689 or 1694. Beginning in 1701, the local community paid taxes to the major *kahal* in Siemiatycze. (However, some sources indicate that the community was not formed until the middle of the 18th century.) In 1878, 460 of the town's

**Mielnik:** *synagogue, now used as retail shop and warehouse (photo TW, 1988)*

1,147 inhabitants were Jews; at the outbreak of World War II, Jews numbered approximately 200.

A brick synagogue on the market square (at Brzeska Street), survived the Holocaust and its aftermath, though today the building houses a shop. You will find the Jewish cemetery, with about 50 *mazevas*, in the northern part of town, next to the chalk factory, on Metna Road. The following *mazevas* have been deciphered: Mordechaj, son of Jakow; Jehuda Lejb Tarek (Turek); and Manes, son of Hirsz Rubin.

Jewish families named in the 1928 guide: "Shops: Halpern Dawid, Lewinson Symcha, Rubin Gershon, Berman Chaim, Kotelman Dawid."

## Milejczyce

*Population 2,636.*

*87 km south of Bialystok and 23 km northeast of Siemiatycze.*

In the 16th century, Milejczyce's Jewish settlers came into conflict with the Christian townsmen. As a result, it was not until the middle of the 16th century that the independent Jewish community was formed there. In 1878, 627 of the town's 1,588 residents were Jews; by 1935 that number had grown to 894.

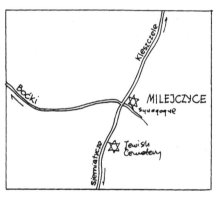

Milejczyce's last rabbi was Aron Izaak Tamares.

On Borowika Street, in the center of town, you will find a large brick synagogue dating from 1927. Serving as both library and cinema in the years since World War II, the structure has been under renovation since 1985. (A lack of funds has slowed that process.) Proceeding to the southern portion of town, you will come across a Jewish cemetery (on Nurzec Road) that was founded in 1865. Several concrete tombstones remain, however none were found with discernible inscriptions.

The following names are those included on the record of the Jewish families taken by the Nazis to death camps. However, these are names only of those families that owned their own

houses; those who lived with other families or with farmers were
not recorded:
   Bacman, Leja; Bejles (Bejlas), Rywka; Betki, Rywa; Berek,
Abram; Berezowski, Symcha Leja Abram; Brezezinski, Rywa;
Boruch, Isaak Abram; Burak, Wolf; Chrabostowski, Josel; Czapka,
Gedali; Dejboch, Sara Josel; Dobryman, Icko; Farber, Liba Hilary
Abram; Gedali, Sachar; Gilnes, Berko; Gorfajn, Motel Tewie
Chajm Lejzer Lejzor; Grynberg, Welwel Dawid; Kac, Malka;
Kaplan, Jankiel; Koc, Chaja; Kostecki, Icko; Krawcow, Icko; Lec,
Chaja Chana Abram; Lew, Herszko; Lewinson, Liba Aram;
Limonski, Moshe; Malmed, Szloma Jowel; Mosieznik, Szepsel;
Nusbaum, Aron; Ochrymski, Oerszko; Oksegron, Bobel; Orlanski,
Szmul; Piekar, Gedali; Piekarski, Pinkus; Popowicz, Eli; Prync,
Rywka; Rabinowicz, Tema; Reznik, Aron; Rozenfarb, Boruch;
Samuil, Lejb; Segal, Josel Icko; Skarbnik, Srul; Smujt, Lejb;
Sokolowski, Jankiel; Strykowski, Wolf; Supel, Susel Szachno
Rubin; Sznajder, Mejer; Szpulanka, Rachel; Szymonowicz, Srul;
Tamares, Aron - rabbi; Tencer, Abram; Tenenbaum, Lejb;
Terespolski, Chaim Naftali; Trostaniecki, Moshe; Turek, Lejb;
Wajnsztajn, Moshe; Wasergat, Leja Senter; Watnik, Eli Aron;
Widzkowski, Srul Abram; Wojnar, Chalka Aron; Wolkowycki,
Maszka Kalman; Wyczolkier, Srul Szloma; Zajac, Jankiel Zelman;
Zaleszanski, Naftali.
   For more information, contact Cezary Okuniewski at 3
Borowika Street (across from the synagogue) who is quite knowl-
edgeable about the Jews who used to live in Milejczyce. He lives
in a former rabbi's house, the attic of which is papered with pre-
war Jewish newspapers.

## Narew

*Population 5,158 (in 1993).*

*42 km southeast of Bialystok.*

The first mention of Jews living in Narew dates back to 1560.
Then, in approximately 1580, some of Narew's Jews were accused
of a ritual murder and were eventually forced—along with all the
other Jewish inhabitants—to leave town. It was not until the
beginning of the 19th century that the community was reestab-
lished. In 1897, 601 of the town's 1,434 inhabitants were Jews, and
by the outbreak of World War II, that number had dwindled to
approximately 300. The town's last rabbis were Ruben Kahan and

Tewie Lejzerowski.
Miraculously, the town's
mid-19th century wooden
synagogue survived the
Holocaust and went on to
function after the war as a
movie house (see photo).
However, the structure was
torn down after a 1973 fire. In
addition, a Jewish cemetery
can be found in the Glinica
Forest near the village of
Makowka. It contains
about 70 *mazevas* that
were recovered in 1983
from Piaski Street curbs
by Jan Topolanski.

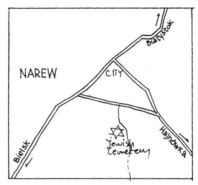

Some of the Jewish
families named in the
1928 guide: "Owners of
shops: Bachrach Judel,
Farber Tanchum,
Kaczalski Icko, Kagan
Symcha, Serlin Abram,
Gerszon Nachum,
Wadman Ruwen."

*Narew: mid-19th century synagogue, used as a
cinema after World War II; torn down after
1973 fire (photo Marian Swiecki, 1970)*

## Narewka

*Population 5,026 (in 1993).*

*68 km southeast of Bialystok.*

The Jews formed their community here at the beginning of the
19th century and by approximately 1880 as many as 778 (or 90
percent) of the town's 863 inhabitants were Jewish. Just prior to
the outbreak of World War II, the town's Jewish residents numbered approximately 899. Their last rabbi was Szajko-Szejko.

During the Soviet occupation of 1939–1941 the wooden synagogue was turned into a grain storehouse, which caused such an
outrage among the Jews that they burned the temple themselves.
The Jewish cemetery, however, remained. Located on a hill on the
Guszczewine road, the burial ground contains 230 *mazevas* and is

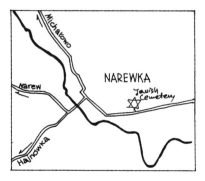

partially surrounded by a stone wall that states that the cemetery was completed just two weeks before the outbreak of World War II—on August 15, 1939. Among the most interesting *mazevas* here is one made of labradorite, a rare stone from the Caucasus and one covered with flakes of gold leaf. Thanks to mem-

*Narewka: Iwona Wisniewska, the author's wife, preparing map of Jewish cemetery (photo TW, 1992)*

bers of the Society of Friends of the Hajnowka Region, several of the *mazevas* here have been properly replaced, and many of them preserved with their original colors.

The following names, with dates of death, were discernible on *mazevas* in this cemetery:

1873 — Cwi Jechijel Halewi
1874 — Abram Cwi Halewi Zfas
1874 — Mordeche Mordechaj
1899 — Szmarje Barylkowski
1913 — Szyfra Gitel Halpern
1918 — Jakow Szmuel, son of Symcha Bagon
1919 — Eli Cyrylnik
1919 — Dawid Grabarski
1919 — Moshe Rejskind
1923 — Hilke Wilder
1925 — Jehuda Lejb Abramski
1926 — Naftali Slonimski
1928 — Mordechaj, son of Icchok Rabinowicz
1928 — Sima Liba Augustower
1929 — Jakow Dow, son of Szlomo Tabacznik

1930 — Chazas Hiel, son of Aron Sapirsztejn
1930 — Liba Rejzel Fabter
1930 — Chana Sztejnberg
1931 — Jehuda Ejdel Barenbojm
1932 — Chasza Fejgiel Epsztajn
1932 — Fejgel Wolanski
1934 — Jowl Eliezer Liberman
1934 — Eliezer Josef Malecki
1935 — Jehoszua Jelin
1935 — David Goldacki
1935 — Cyryl Milecki Malecki
No date — Tenenbaum (no first name)
1936 — Josif Biszke Kaflanski
1936 — Bejla, daughter of Szlomo Szapiro
1938 — Aron Otensztejn
No date — Schmidt Szmuel Mordechaj
No date — Fejga Sztejn
Meir reb Rafael Bielski Elken Bazelski
Menachem Szlomo Grabarski or Grobodzki
Szyfra Gitel, daughter of Jehoszua Halpern

The fate of the Jews from Narewka and other settlements near the extensive Bialowieza Forest (Hajnowka, Bialowieza, Szereszewo) was determined by the location of these settlements (residents were considered a potential source of support for resistance fighters who could hide in the forest). Narewka Jews were the first in the region to be murdered. Near the Christian cemetery on the northern side of the railroad tracks is a commemorative plaque with the following inscription: "Common grave of 300 Jewish people murdered by the Nazis on the 5th of August, 1941. Honor to their memory."

For more information about the history of Jews from Narewka, contact former resident Wiktor Kabac, who now lives in nearby Hajnowka at 421 Lakowa Street (telephone 2254), or Nadzieja Sakowska at 55 Mickiewicza Street in Narewka.

# *Orla*

*Population 4,548 (in 1993).*

*63 km south of Bialystok and 12 km southeast of Bielsk.*

Jews could be found in Orla as far back as the 16th century, at the end of which the independent community was formed. By 1616, the town included 17 Jewish houses and a synagogue, and by 1676, approximately half the town's inhabitants were Jews (104). In 1897, 2,310 (or 77 percent) of the town's 3,003 inhabitants were Jews. Just prior to the outbreak of World War II, approximately 1,500 Jews lived in Orla. The town's last rabbi was Eli Halpern.

A magnificent brick synagogue as well as the remains of the Jewish cemetery survived World War II. No one has been able to assign a precise date to the synagogue's construction: Some sources put it in the second quarter of the 17th century, while others—including historian K. Kaczynski—place its construction at the end of the 18th century. Legend has it that Jews bought a former Calvinist temple from the Radziwill family for 10,000 groshen. Supposedly, the Jews had been asking Duchess Radziwill to sell this otherwise useless temple for such a long time that she finally agreed to it, though only on the condition that they bring her the 10,000 groshen in 1-groshen coins! In 1926 the synagogue burned but was quickly rebuilt by the Orla Jews. Unfortunately, though, the fire consumed a magnificent *Aron ha-Kodesh* Ark. (Luckily, it was photographed in 1916 by Herman Struck, so a record of it does exist.) During World War II, the synagogue was used as a hospital and a warehouse; after the war, it

gradually fell into decline. Since 1983, however, it has been under almost constant reconstruction. In 1994 the building was covered by a new roof, but further renovation came to a halt for lack of funds. There was talk of converting the building

*Orla: the Great Synagogue, now restored (photo Jan Glinka, 1935; collection TW)*

into a cultural center but it seems unlikely to happen in the near future.

Next to the main synagogue, prior to World War II, stood two smaller synagogues, as if standing guard. Behind the eastern wall there was a cemetery, though by the beginning of the 19th century it was closed and today has disappeared entirely.

By the Orlanka, you will find the remains of the second Jewish cemetery, which contains approximately 40 *mazevas.* (The majority of tombstones were used to build the road to Bielsk Podlaski.)

To find out more about the Jews in Orla, you can visit Eliasz Oldziejewicz, who lives in a house near the synagogue and for years has looked after it.

The State Archives in Bialystok contain birth and marriage certificates of Orla Jews dating from 1836. In addition, the November 18, 1990, Belarussian-language weekly *Niva* (edited in Bialystok) contains a description of a prewar Jewish wedding ceremony held in Orla.

Jewish families named in the 1928 guide: "Owners of shops: Rabinowicz Moshe, Bertman Symcha, Klementynowski Gershon, Kestin Hirsz, Szapiro Szymon, Cymbal Michael, Golde Aharon, Goniadzki Kalman, Gruskin Dawid, Tenenbaum Judel."

## *Siemiatycze*

*Population 14,992 (in 1993).*

*99 km south of Bialystok, via Highway 19.*

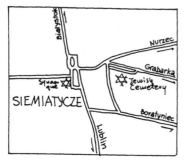

Jews were living in Siemiatycze as early as 1582, and kahal are mentioned as far back as 1653. In 1765 the town's Jewish population numbered 1,015, more than twice that of Bialystok at the time. The 1897 census set that number at 4,636, or 75 percent of the town's total population of 6,000. At the outbreak of the World War II, that number had dwindled to approximately 4,000. The last rabbi here was Baruch Gersztejn.

*Siemiatycze: 18th-century stamp of court of Jewish community (collection TW)*

Siemiatycze is in a way the birthplace of Zionism, because it was here in the 18th century that the idea originated as Gedali set out to convince his fellow Jews of the necessity of re-creating their former state. Gedali, along with his brother Moses, traveled to Palestine as early as 1700, and in 1716 he published "A Prayer for Peace in Jerusalem" in Berlin. In 1897, at the Congress in Basel, Theodor Herzl formally presented the theory of Zionism; however, it was Siemiatycze's Gedali who had originally promoted the idea 200 years earlier.

Until almost the middle of the last century, the Eastern Orthodox community of Siemiatycze celebrated the "Evening of Zalman" in connection with its own Easter celebration. Legend has it that Jews were once the leaseholders of Russian Orthodox churches; thus if the faithful wanted to pray, they had to ask the Jews for the keys to the Russian Orthodox temple. A puppet-like figure of Zalman was taken outside the city, where the faithful then had to request that he turn over the keys. Since Zalman never replied, the request seemingly ignored, the Orthodox faithful would then grow angry and throw themselves on the puppet, tearing it to pieces. All of this took place to the accompaniment of comical cries and teasing of Zalman.

A brick synagogue, a Talmudic house, and the gate and decorated wall of the Polna Street cemetery (see photos on next page) are the only Jewish structures to have survived World War II. At the cemetery you will find a plaque commemorating 73 murdered Jews (though the inscription mentions only three by name: Efroim Kejles, Abram Ekstrakt, and Mejta Lew). Not a single prewar *mazeva* can be found at this site, though several can be traced to the foundations of a house across the street from the cemetery wall, as well as the stairs of a wooden building between the Gmina Office (County Office) and the high school on Kosciuszki Street, about one km from the cemetery (see photo on next page).

## Some Views in Siemiatycze

*Interior of the Great Synagogue (photo Herman Struck, 1916; courtesy Moshe Verbin)*

*The Great Synagogue, 1926 (photo Jankiel Tykocki; courtesy Jerzy Nowicki)*

*Gate of the Jewish cemetery; no grave markers remain here, only a post-World War II memorial plaque (photo TW, 1988)*

*Gravestone from Jewish cemetery, now used as a stair step near school on Kosciuszki Street (photo TW, 1989)*

*Great Synagogue shortly after World War II; a museum today (photographer unknown, collection TW)*

*Talmudic house near Great Synagogue, now a kindergarten (photo TW, 1988)*

The main synagogue, at 1 Zaszkolna Street, was built in the Classical style between 1755 and 1779 and was based on the design of the well-known architect Szymon Bogumil Zuga (see photos on page 99). Special washstands were gifts to the Jews from the owner of the town, Duchess Anna Jablonowska, while a decorated small column with a collection box was the offering of Baron Meizner. Women entered the gallery through a balustrade. During their occupation, the Germans looted the building and used it as a warehouse. After 1944, whatever remained of the valuable interior, including the *bimah* and a wooden *Aron ha-Kodesh*, was destroyed. Between 1961 and 1964, the building was renovated, and today it houses a cultural center and a museum. Inside is a plaque with the following inscription: "To the memory of the Jewish community of Siemiatycze, which shared the town's vicissitudes for more than four centuries." The museum also contains a unique collection of pictures by the 20th-century artist Jozef Charyton, who uses as his subjects the Jews of the Bialystok region. Next to the former synagogue is the Talmudic house Talmud-Torah. Built in about 1915, the structure today functions as a kindergarten (see photo on page 99).

In addition to these Jewish structures, the town contains several other architecturally interesting buildings, including a 17th-century church and monastery, and a Protestant chapel. There also remains a sphinx at the gate where once stood the palace of Duchess Anna Sapieha Jablonowska. She was a supporter of local Jews and died in 1801.

If you wish to learn more about the history of Siemiatycze, you should seek out the town's passionate historian and editor of the local newspaper, *Glos Siemiatycz* (Voice of Siemiatycze), Jerzy Nowicki, at 6 Plac Wyzwolenia-Rynek (telephone 552656, or 556131). At his newspaper office many tourist guides and brochures are available for purchase.

## Grabarka

*10 km east of Siemiatcz.*

From Siemiatycze it is a short journey to the Holy Mountain in Grabarka. To reach Grabarka, simply follow Wysoka Street (near the Jewish cemetery) or Armii Krajowej Street toward Boratyniec village. The Holy Mountain in Grabarka is the spiritual capital of the Eastern Orthodox faith in Poland. Here, among the trees, stands the only orthodox nunnery in all of Poland, and adjacent to it on a hill stands a church surrounded by some 15,000 wooden crosses brought by pilgrims. On each August 19th—the Day of the Transfiguration of the Savior—some 20,000 pilgrims and visitors from all over the world come to Grabarka.

## Sokolka

*Population 19,872 (in 1993).*

*41 km northeast of Bialystok, via Highway 18.*

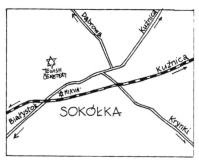

Jews settled in Sokolka in the second half of the 17th century, and in 1698, they received from King Sigismundus Augustus II the privilege to build a synagogue and found a cemetery here. However, the Jewish community in Sokolka acknowledged the jurisdiction of the Grodno kahal until the end of the 18th century. Although Sokolka's Jewish population grew continuously throughout the years, it never exceeded 50 percent of the total population, a rarity in the Bialystok region. In 1897, 2,848 (or 37 percent) of the town's 7,596 residents were Jews, and by the outbreak of World War II approximately 3,000 Jews lived in Sokolka. Their last rabbis were Berko Srulewicz Fridberg and Icko Szuster.

Tragically, none of Sokolka's five synagogues survived the Holocaust and its aftermath. The main brick synagogue (erected around 1900) was pulled down after the war and its foundations used to build a school (on Szkolna Street, in the southwestern part of the city). However, a Jewish *mykva* still survives (at the corner of Sienna and

*Road sign pointing to village of Palestyna (photo WT, 1995)*

## Some Views of Sokolka

*Information sign at Jewish cemetery
(photo TW, 1989)*

*Graves in Jewish cemetery, before
World War II (photographer unknown;
collection TW)*

*Gravestone with lion symbol (photo TW,
1989)*

*Jewish ritual bath, now an apart-
ment house (photo TW, 1988)*

Kwiatowa Streets), as does a
Jewish cemetery that sits atop a
small hill on Zamenhofa Street (in
the northwestern part of town).
Generally protected by local
inhabitants, the cemetery retains a
stone wall and approximately
1,000 *mazevas*, some with interesting symbols and inscriptions.
The oldest identified *mazeva* dates from 1751. The following
names, together with dates of death, are those that can be deciphered on the *mazevas* here:

1907 — Ester Fejga Blumental
1911 — Josef, son of Icchok Kohen Fuks
1912 — Mordechaj, son of Beniamin Orlowicz
1919 — David, son of Abraham Sztachinski Sztabinski

1919 — Israel Jakow Gerszon Halewi Lewin
1928 — Szymon David Tynski
1935 — Pesza, daughter of Israel Mordechaj Mudchen Widocka
1940 — Jejsef Kadysz Biebrich
No date —Ester, daughter of Moshe Kalman Halpern

Moshe Verbin was born in Sokolka in 1920. He has lived for many years in the kibbutz Yakum in Israel, where he has been building models (on the scale 1:100) of the wooden synagogues — mostly from the Bialystok region—once so prevalent in Poland and thus preserving for future generations a special record of Eastern Europe. His work has been exhibited in shows around the world.

Sokolka is quite near to a village named Palestine ("Palestyna"). Once home to a community of Jewish farmers, the village of Palestyna was one of three colonies in the Sokolka area settled by Jewish farmers in 1850. Twenty-six farmers started Kolonia Izaaka (Isaac's Colony) near Odelsk (today part of Belarus), while 10 settlers started the colony Chanaan, and six, Palestine. Thus today, in Poland, between the villages of Bilminy and Nomiki, a tiny settlement remains with the odd-sounding name, Palestyna (see photo on page 101).

Close to Palestyna is the Tartar village of Bohoniki. Tartars settled in the area nearly 300 years ago, after the victory of King John III Sobieski in the 1683 battle of Vienna. Both this village and the Tartar village of Kruszyniany (near Krynki) are noteworthy for their wooden mosques (the only wooden mosques in Europe) and their Muslim cemeteries. A Tartar museum is located in the center of Sokolka, and each February the mosque villages are the site of celebrations during the month-long Ramadan observance.

## Suchowola

*Population 8,132 (in 1993).*

*53 km north of Bialystok, via Highway 19.*

Jews arrived in this town—the geographical center of Europe—at the beginning of the 17th century, and in 1698 received settlement privileges from King Sigismundus Augustus II. By 1897, 1,944 (or 60 percent) of the town's 3,203 residents were Jews. At the out-

*Suchowola: wooden synagogue, 1936; no longer standing (photo Szymon Zajczyk; courtesy Institute of Art PAN, Warsaw)*

break of World War II approximately 1,500 Jews lived here, including the last rabbi, Szlome Cwi Kalir.

Of the town's two synagogues, the most famous (built of wood) was destroyed in the war (see photo at left), and the other (built of brick) was so completely rebuilt that its original appearance is barely discernible. (The building is now used as a school.) The Jewish cemetery is located in the northern portion of town, in the forest by the Olszanka River; however, only rubble remains.

Jewish families named in the 1928 guide: "Brewery: Grodzienski Mendel; Photographer: Lewin Judel; Tea-bistro: Charlap Mendel; Bakeries: Eberstein Icko, Chinski Lejb, Lewin Mendel, Szuster Ruben."

## Suprasl

*Population 4,405 (in 1993).*

*15 km northeast of Bialystok, via Highway 676.*

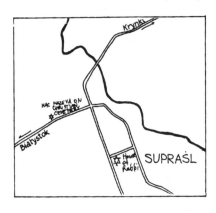

Prior to World War II, this small town could have served as a model for the peaceful cohabitation of various ethnic and religious groups. The funeral of Baroness Bucholz, for example, was attended by a Russian Orthodox priest, a Roman Catholic priest, and a rabbi—all of whom stood beside the leading Protestant preacher. And the construction of the Suprasl synagogue was financed by a member of the German Bucholz family, who offered Rabbi Subotnik 500 rubles.

Suprasl's Jewish community was established at the beginning of the 19th century. By 1897, 466 of the town's 2,459 inhabitants were Jews. However, just prior to the outbreak of World War II, that number had fallen to about 300. Suprasl's last rabbi was Awigdor Rabinowicz.

Suprasl never had its own Jewish cemetery; instead, its Jewish residents buried their dead in the Bialystok cemetery. However, visitors to the Suprasl Protestant cemetery can see a *mazeva* there that has been converted into a Christian tombstone, the stone probably taken from the Jewish cemetery in Bialystok. Although Suprasl's brick synagogue did not survive the War, the rabbi's house—at 11 Listopada Street—is still standing.

Despite its lack of material remnants from its Jewish past, Suprasl is worth visiting for the simple reason that it is one of the most appealing towns in the Bialystok region. (Local authorities have attempted to acquire spa status for the town.) Located on the Suprasl River, the town is home to a monastery, and work is presently underway to rebuild one of the oldest and most interesting Eastern Orthodox churches in Poland. In the center of town, the former Bucholz family manor is now a well-regarded, regional art school.

For more information about the town and its history, contact artist and sculptor Wojciech Zaleski, who works at the art school and lives at 32 Cegielna Street (telephone 183085). Another potential source of information is Leonard Dobrowolski (12 Slowackiego Street), who has written about the Suprasl Jews in the local newspaper. In addition, you will find a good collection of materials about prewar Suprasl at the Knyszyn Forest Museum. It is on the eastern edge of Suprasl and is well worth the visit.

The following Jewish names are recorded in the Suprasl registry for 1909:

Biber, Bera; Blacher, Jankiel; Butynski, Chackiel; Calewicz, Jankiel; Chazan, Isar; Elson, Lejb; Epsztejn, Mowsiej; Glazer, Hersz; Goldschmidt, Lejzer; Goldstein, Lejb; Goldszodt, Jankiel; Grynszpan, Moshe; Gutkiewica, Tauba; Kagan, Szolem; Kaplan, Tauba; Linderbaum, Samuel; Lemberg, Moshe; Kaplanski, Judke; Ojtenstein, Abram; Rotenberg, Mejer.

## Su_raz

*Population 1,022 (in 1993).*

*23 km southwest of Bialystok and 9 km southeast of Lapy.*

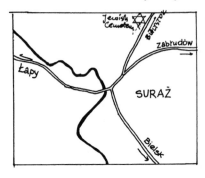

Visitors to Suraz today will find it difficult to believe that this, the smallest town in the Bialystok region, was formerly the area's largest and richest town, and home to a castle and several temples.

The town was founded in 1445 and Suraz's first Jews date as far back as 1525. Later in the 16th century, the townsmen obtained the royal privilege "De Non Tolerandis Judaeis," and the Jews of Suraz were forced to leave. It was not until the end of the 18th century that a Jewish community was once again established here. By 1897, 366 of the town's 1,599 residents were Jews. Just prior to the Holocaust, about 15 Jewish families resided here.

A small Jewish cemetery with 10 *mazevas* survives today in the northeastern portion of town. Founded in 1865 (although a *mazeva* dating from 1792 has been deciphered, possibly moved from an older cemetery), the Suraz Jewish cemetery is surrounded by a stone wall. The following are the names, with date of death, which could be translated from the tombstones in this cemetery:

1800 — Golda, daughter of Dow
1885 — Lea, daughter of Jakub Halewi
1885 — Fruma Amiel, daughter of Israel
1916 — Moshe Ben Rabi and his wife
1926 — Cwi, son of Dow
No date —Son of Zew Aaron Baluch

One other site worth visiting in Suraz is Wladislaw Litwinczuk's "open-air museum of the earth." Housed in the courtyard of a private apartment building, the museum's collection includes thousands of old tools as well as household utensils dating from centuries ago. The museum is located in the center of the city, on the main street leading to Bialystok.

## Wasilkow

*Population 7,272 (in 1993).*

*8 km north of Bialystok, via Highway 18.*

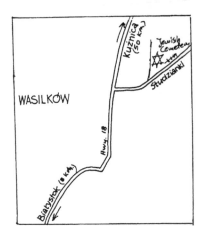

Founded as a town in 1566, Wasilkow received its first Jewish settlers sometime prior to 1653, and by 1714 a Jewish community had been formed. In 1897, 1,470 of the town's 3,800 inhabitants were Jews. At the outbreak of World War II, approximately 1,000 Jews resided here. Until 1935, the rabbi was Rafael Gordon, followed by Israel Halpern, whose sons, Jakow and Szmuel Halpern, also held titles of rabbis.

Wasilkow is best known for the water system built there in 1890–92 to provide the city of Bialystok with water. Close to the town there is a site called Holy Water on which sits a Roman Catholic church and a spring of supposedly miraculous water.

None of Wasilkow's synagogues survived the Holocaust; in 1941 the Nazis torched its 18th-century synagogue (shown in photo below). Of the town's three Jewish cemeteries, only one

**Wasilkow:** *18th-century wooden synagogue, destroyed in 1941 (photographer unknown; courtesy Anthony Rudolph)*

**Wasilkow:** *sign at entrance to Jewish cemetery (photo TW, 1995)*

*Zabludow: 17th-century wooden synagogue, c. 1930; destroyed in the Holocaust (photo Szymon Zajczyk; collection TW)*

remains. With 13 *mazevas*, it is on the road to Dabrowka village on Slowackiego Street (sign at entrance shown in photo on next page).

The following names, with date of death, are those decipherable on *mazevas* in the cemetery:

1886 — Chana, daughter of Metel, killed by Szlojme Arie
1886 — Haszewa Katzner
1910 — Ajsza Gitel Raszkies, daughter of Josef
1913 — Israel Nachum, son of Chaim Pokrzewiec
1913 — Dwora Polak
1915 — Rasze, daughter of Nacum Fink
1917 — Leja, daughter of Ratner Ratznera Rachel
1919 — Jakow Mordechaj, son of Meir Gite
1922 — Sara Kadisz

## Zabludow

*Population 2,153 (in 1993).*

*20 km northeast of Bialystok, via Highway 19.*

Historical evidence points to the presence of Jews in Zabludow as early as the 1520s. The Jewish community was formed in 1566, and in 1635 Jews acquired the privilege to found a cemetery and build a synagogue. The 1897 census indicates that as many as 2,621 (or 70 percent) of the town's 3,772 inhabitants were Jews. By the outbreak of World War II, that number had fallen to approximately 2,000. The town's last rabbi was Joachan Mirsky.

The Holocaust destroyed not only the Jews of Zabludow but also their world-famous wooden synagogue that dated from the 17th century (see photo above). Employing a unique construction, the larch wood temple included not a single nail. Although the synagogue itself has disappeared, the building's plan and full documentation are still available, holding out hope that somewhere financing will be found for the ongoing efforts to rebuild this masterpiece of wooden Jewish architecture.

The old Jewish cemetery was also destroyed during the last war, though a fragment of another cemetery remains in the southwestern portion of town. Nameless concrete tombs lie by the country road, and above this landscape of destruction towers an obelisk (*ohel*) like a monument to the annihilated Jewish nation. The *ohel* was built on the grave of the tzaddik rabbi Icchok, son of Cwi Dow Ber, born in New York, who died and was buried in Zabludow in 1927. The efforts of the local community resulted in the cemetery's recently being surrounded by a stone wall.

Jewish families named in the 1928 guide:

"Textiles: Fajman, M.; builders: Goldfarb, Mr.; bricks: Narewski, B.; wood: Wagman, G.L.H.: tannery: Beker, J.M.; Hellersztejn, Miller Ch.; Pleban, F.; Rubin, Z.; Bartelski, G.; smiths: Bartnowski, I.; Miesionczuk, J.; Wolf, F.; tailors: Gladsztejn, L.; mills: Czesler, J.; Milner, T.; bakers: Zabludowski, M.; Beker, Gordzienski; Cymerman, R.; Pune, M.; leather: Asz, L.; Bachrach, A.; Epsztejn, D.; Szeps, J.; grocers: Brencer; Intoligator, Ch.; Kadysz, S.; Kornzer, S.; Mendelson, J.; shoemaker: Perelgut, M.; watchmaker: Markus; Irons: Miesiecznik, Lewin A."

To obtain more information about prewar Zabludow, contact Jan Leonczuk (telephone 188175). A poet, teacher, and village administrator of Lubniki, near Zabludow, Leonczuk has been collecting information about Zabludow's history for years.

## Appendix I

## A *Chronology of Jewish Life in Bialystok*

**1463–1487:** The first Jews settle in Podlasie, a portion of which later came to be called *Bialostocczyzna*, or the Bialystok region.

**1514:** First historical mention of Bialystok.

**1522:** Tykocin becomes home to the region's first Jewish community.

**1558:** The first Jews arrive in Bialystok (according to Tykocin records).

**1659:** Bialystok Jews acknowledge the authority of the Tykocin *kahal*.

**1715–1718:** The Nomer Tamid Society sponsors the construction of Old Beth Hamidrash, the town's first brick synagogue.

**1745:** Bialystok Jews receive full rights of citizenship.

**1750:** Joshua Shapiro becomes rabbi of Bialystok and Choroszcz.

**1763:** The City Hall (Rathaus) Clock Tower erected in the center of Bialystok.

**1764:** Alte Szul, the Great Synagogue, is constructed.

**1771–1777:** Bialystok's Jewish community becomes autonomous (no longer under Tykocin's jurisdiction).

**1779:** Bialystok becomes part of Prussia.

**1789:** Rabbi Gaon Klonimus Kalman Lichtensztejn—the third rabbi of Bialystok and the first of the independent *kahal*—dies.

**1800:** Naje Beth Midrash constructed on Shulhof Street. The towns of Janow, Jasionowka, Knyszyn, Choroszcz, Grodek, Odelsk, Sokolka, Zabludow, and Wasilkow all acknowledge the jurisdiction of the Bialystok *kahal*.

**1803–1804:** Aron Lewi Hurwic opens Bialystok's first Jewish printing office, which specializes in Hebrew editions of religious books .

**1807:** After a brief occupation by Napoleon's army, Bialystok becomes part of Russia.

**1810:** Chaim Zelig Slonimski, founder of the Hebrew periodical *Hacefira*, is born in Bialystok.

**1812:** Bialystok reverts to French hegemony.

**1815:** Bialystok is returned to the Russian state.

**1816:** Political activist Szmuel Salan is born in Bialystok. (In 1851 he settled in Jerusalem and became one of the founders of the city Petah Tikwa.)

**1821:** Hewre Kadisha is founded.

**1826:** Bikur Chojlim (a philanthropic organization) is founded.

**1828:** Gemillus Chasodim—which later became the Linas Hatsedek—is established.

**1830:** Home for Chronically Ill is founded.

**1833:** Eleazar Halbersztadt, founder of Bialystok's *Haskala* movement, settles in the town. He died in 1899.

**1840:** First Jewish hospital founded in Bialystok by Sender Alexander Bloch. (He also established the town's first textile factory in 1842.)

**1850:** Mochum Minc and Sender Bloch establish the first silk factory in Bialystok.

**1855:** Kasryel Kaplan and Gwirc establish the first Jewish comprehensive school.

**1859:** Esperanto creator Ludwik Zamenhof is born. The first stage of the railroad from Warsaw to St. Petersburg via Bialystok is completed.

**1861:** Tzar Alexander II visits Bialystok and receives the delegation of Jechijel Ber Wolkowyski, Eleazer Halbersztad, Dawid and Mordechaj Zabludowski, and Rabbi Johoszue Szejnberg.

**1862:** Pulkowaja Beth Midrash opens. Philologist and writer Leo Wiener is born. (Died in 1939 after becoming a noted professor in the United States.)

**1863:** Jewish Hospital moves to a new building funded by industrialist Icchok Zabludowski.

**1867–1873:** Chorshul synagogue constructed.

**1876:** Mejer Wallach (later Maxim Litwinov) foreign minister of the USSR from 1930 to 1939, is born in Bialystok to a prominent *Hasidim* family. From 1940 to 1943, he served as Soviet Ambassador to the United States. Wallach died in Moscow in 1951.

**1878:** Josef Perlman is born in Bialystok. He created in Bialystok and later in Moscow the Habimah Theater, the first Hebrew Theater in Europe. Today Habimah is the National Theatre in Israel.

**1882:** First strike of Jewish weavers. First pogrom. The political party Hovei Zion is formed. Jechijel Ber Wolkowyskier opens Jewish Home for the Elderly.

**1883:** Rabbi Szmuel Mohilever arrives in Bialystok. A kosher canteen for Jewish soldiers is organized through the initiative of Oszer Topolski and Szmuel Rapaport.

**1885:** The medical and charitable organization Linas Hatsedek is created. Poet and journalist Zusman Segalowicz is born.

**1891:** Jewish cemetery opened in the Bagnowka district .

**1895:** Eliezer Ber Lieberman—father of Aron Lieberman, one of the founders of Jewish socialist movement—dies in Bialystok.

**1896:** Major fire in Bialystok. First horse-drawn streetcars begin operating.

**1897:** Gynecologist Josif Rubinsztejn settles in Bialystok and organizes bund. Dr. Josef Chazanowicz, Dr. Lipman Rozental, Dawid Suchowolski, and Josif Mohilever attend First Congress of Zionism in Basel, Switzerland.

**1898:** Szmuel Mohilever dies; Rabbi Chain Herz Halpern takes over his office.

**1899:** Fire brigade is formed, Jews make up 90 percent of the force. Well-known ophthamologist Leon Pines settles in Bialystok. The first illegal bund paper—*The Worker of Bialystok*—is printed in Yiddish.

**1900:** Jewish business people found Trade School.

**1902:** Szmuel Beth Midrash synagogue is established.

**1903:** The Poale Sijon party is formed.

**1905:** Pejsach Kaplan and Noach Zabludowski start the Jewish Art organization. On August 12 the Russian army incites a pogrom in which 36 Jews are murdered.

**1906:** Bialystok representatives Abraham Tyktin, Dr. Tuvia Cytron, Dr. Josif Mohilever, Falk Kempner, Dr. Mojzesz Perelsztejn, and Dr. Alexander Rajgrodzki are elected to the Russian Parliament (Duma). On June 1 through June 3 another pogrom takes place in Bialystok; this time 110 Jews are killed.

**1908:** The new Great Synagogue is opened.

**1909:** The Jewish newspaper *Golos Bielastoka* (in Russian) appears.

**1912:** The Jewish Palace theater is opened in Bialystok. The first Jewish kindergarten begins operating.

**1913:** Habima theater group is formed, and under the direction of Nachum Cemach, Osip Dymow's "Szma Israel" is performed in a translation by Pejsach Kaplan. S. Herszberg serves as editor of Bialystok's first daily newspaper, *Bialystoker Tageblatt*.

**1919:** Edited by Pejsach Kaplan, the daily *Dos Naje Lebn* (which after 1931 became *Unzern Lebn*) begins publication. The Szolem Alejchem Library is opened on May 13. The first Jewish Art Exhibition takes place, including the work of Jankiel Adler.

**1920:** The Hebrew Gymnasium is founded. Dr. Gedali Rozenman is appointed rabbi of the city. David Sohn comes to Bialystok, bringing $140,000 from the Bialystoker Relief Committee in New York.

**1921:** First Polish census in Bialystok reports 76,792 residents, of whom 39,603 are Jews.

**1923:** The journalist Nachum Sokolov (1859 - 1936) visits Bialystok to cover the First Zionist Congress.

**1925:** The first bus makes its way to Bialystok.

**1926:** The Jewish theater "Gilarino" is created.

**1928:** The ambulance service of Linas Hatsedek begins operation.

**1929:** Judel Kalecki, the founder of the Crafts School, dies. Tuberculosis Sanatorium opens in a building donated by Fani Trilling.

**1931:** Pejsach Kaplan opens the Library of Studies (library of Jewish Community)

**1932:** Jakow Berman, well-known conductor and composer for synagogue "Chorshul" dies.

**1933:** Hechalutz (an organization preparing young people for emigration to Palestine) hold its conference in Bialystok. Visit of David Ben Gurion, Prime Minister of Israel (1949 to 1963).

**1941:** On June 27, the Germans enter Bialystok. On August 1, they create and fence in the ghetto.

**1942:** On November 2, the Nazis liquidate all of the Jewish communities (ghettoes) in the Bialystok province except Bialystok, Jasionowka, and parts of Krynki and Sokolka. About 100,000 Jews of the Bialystok region are transferred to death camps in Treblinka, Majdanek, and Oswiecim, where they are killed.

**1943:** On January 24 and 25, the ghettoes in Jasionowka, Krynki, and Sokolka are liquidated. From February 5 through February 12, the Nazis transfer approximately 10,000 Jews from the Bialystok ghetto to death camps in Treblinka and Oswieim.

**1943:** On August 16 an uprising takes place in the Jewish ghetto of Bialystok. After several days of fighting that culminate in the death of several thousand Jews in the city area, the last trainload of Jews is sent to Majdanek. On November 3, the Nazis murder Bialystok's 20,000 remaining Jews. According to the historian Szymon Datner the Nazis murdered approximately 240,000 Jews from the Bialystok region (including Grodno), roughly 50,000 of whom were from the city of Bialystok.

**1948:** On February 29, the Jewish Cultural Society is founded and begins operating a library that comes to contain 2,100 books. At the end of this year, there were approximately 520 Jews in Bialystok.

**1971:** The Jewish Ghetto cemetery at Zabia Street is destroyed.

**1993:** The reconstruction and dedication of the obelisk at the site of the Jewish Ghetto cemetery at Zabia Street.

**1997:** Five Jews live in Bialystok.

# APPENDIX II

## Notable Bialystok Jews

Bialystok's Jews were active in all aspects of Bialystok life, especially the intellectual and spiritual realms. In fact, in the period between World War I and World War II, more than 50 newspapers and periodicals were published in Bialystok (as compared to 18 in Lublin and 37 in Cracow). The following biographical notes relate primarily to individuals who are given less attention elsewhere in the book. They are listed in alphabetical order.

**Beker, Israel (1917- ):** Actor, director, writer, and painter, Israel Beker was born in 1917 on Suraska Street, in the heart of Jewish Bialystok. While in the Landsberg camp in Germany, he made and appeared in the feature film *Lang ist der Weg* in Yiddish, which was based on his own script. In 1947 he moved to Palestine. The recipient of many awards, Beker was one of the most esteemed actors and directors in the Habima theater. In the introduction to a book *Stage of Life* (Israel, 1979) in which his paintings appear, Beker writes, "My beginnings are in Bialystok. Do you know where to look for it? It is such a Jewish town between Warsaw and Minsk. A large town. Had my youth been spent elsewhere, my adult life would probably have taken a different course. I am not 'from Bialystok'; I am 'a Bialystoker,' and that means much more. . ."

**Ben, Cijon Rabinowicz (1905-1989):** Considered one of the best religious painters. Benn—as he came to be known—lived most of his adult life in Paris. His father, Szlojme Jakow, designed the Main Synagogue in Bialystok.

**Chazanowicz, Josef (1844-1919):** Born in Grodno, he lived for many years in Bialystok, where a street was named after him. A physician, he went on to create the National and University Library of the State of Israel, which is today named after him.

**Datner, Szymon (1902-1993):** Teacher in the Hebrew Gymnasium in Bialystok. Fought in the Bialystok ghetto uprising. After the war, was Vice President of the Jewish Community in Poland. Author of several books.

**Dymov, Osip (Jozef Perelsztajn) (1878-1959):** Together with Nachum Cemach (born in Bialystok in 1887), Osip formed the

Bialystok Hebrew theater company Habimah in 1912. This theater, which later moved to Moscow, eventually became the National Theater of Israel.

**Grossman, Chajka (1919-1994):** Fought in the Bialystok ghetto. First elected to the Knesset (the Israeli Parliament) in 1969, Chaika became Deputy Speaker of the Knesset in 1986. He wrote a book, *The Underground Army: Fighters of the Bialystok Ghetto*, New York, 1985 (Hebrew edition published in Israel in 1965).

**Halbersztadt, Eleazar (1808-1899):** Grandson of the well-known Rabbi Aarie Eli Hernic from Stanislawow. Eleazar came to Bialystok in 1833 and was highly influential in the development of *Haskala*—Jewish Enlightenment.

**Herszberg, Abraham Samuel (1891-1943):** A respected writer and Jewish historian, Herszberg organized and published the Yiddish *Bialystoker Tageblatt*. This former resident of Kupiecka (Malmeda) Street also organized a Hebrew Language Society before perishing in the liquidation of the ghetto in 1943. His sons in the United States published his monograph about Bialystok in 1949–50. The two-volume *Pinkos Bialistok* is a major source of information about the Jewish people of Bialystok.

**Kaplan, Pesach (1870-1943):** This chief editor of the dailies *Unzer Lebn* and *Dos Naje Lebn* was also a historian, musicologist, correspondent (for the Warsaw newspaper *Moment* and the American *Jewish Daily Forward*), translator (for example, Krylov's fables), and writer. The founder and president of the Jewish People's Party, Kaplan died in the Bialystok ghetto in 1943. The diary of his life in the ghetto, together with other important documents, was subsequently found and published in Poland and the United States.

**Melamed, Leo (1932- ):** Chairman and CEO of Sakura Dellsher, Inc., in Chicago, and chairman emeritus of the Chicago Mercantile Exchange (CME). As chairman of the CME, Melamed introduced foreign currency futures in 1972 with the launching of the International Money Market (IMM)—the first futures market for financial instruments. Under his 25 years of leadership, the CME was transformed from a secondary domestic agricultural exchange to the world's foremost financial futures exchange. In 1984, Melamed spearheaded the concept of international linkages among exchanges by linking the CME to the Singapore International Monetary Exchange (SIMEX). Melamed extended this concept in 1987 by introducing GLOBEX, the world's first electronic futures after-hours trading system, developed in conjunction with Reuters Holdings PLC. He was the first chairman of the National Futures Association, a self-regulatory body of the industry, and continues to serve as its permanent Special Advisor. An attorney by profession, Melamed has lectured and written extensively about financial futures markets, and is the author of a science fiction novel. The University of Chicago Graduate School of Business has established an endowed professorship in his name, and he is a director of the United States Holocaust Memorial Museum.

**Mohilever, Szmuel (1824-1898):** The greatest rabbi of Bialystok (from 1883). Mohilever supported the Zionist movement. Was one of the leaders of Hovevei Zion in Russia. Was a friend of Teodor Herzl (1860-1904), creator of the Zionist political movement. Today many streets in Israel are named after him.

**Ney (Nejman), Nora (1904?-):** Born in a house on Czysta Street in Bialystok, Nora Ney was one of the greatest Polish movie actresses during the period between the wars.

**Pisar, Samuel (1931- ):** Born on Dabrowskiego Street in Bialystok, Pisar was an inhabitant of the Bialystok ghetto and then later of the death camps at Auschwitz, Blizin, Majdanek and Treblinka. Although his family was murdered, he miraculously survived, and went on to a notable career in law and government. He is the author of *Co-Existence and Commerce* (McGraw-Hill, 1970) and the memoir *Of Blood and Hope* (Little, Brown, 1980). He is a practicing international lawyer with offices in New York and Paris.

**Rajrodzki, Aleksander (1877-1943):** Highly regarded physician and deputy mayor of Bialystok who was killed in the Bialystok ghetto.

**Ratner, Max (1909-1995):** Born in Bialystok, he became a successful U.S. businessman and a philanthropist. Ratner for many years supported the Bialystoker Center in New York City and the newspaper *Bialystoker Sztimme*. In addition, he wrote a book of memoirs entitled *The Ratner Family Album* (1990).

**Reines, Frederick, (1918- ):** Born in Paterson, New Jersey, to Bialystok native parents, this physicist was on the staff of the Los Alamos Laboratory before joining the faculty of the University of California in 1966. He shared with another American the Nobel Prize in Physics for 1995.

**Rosario, Rosa (Bursztyn) (1893-1972):** Nicknamed "Amber Rose," from her maiden name, which means "amber" in Polish.

An opera singer for whom Puccini created some memorable roles. Married to another opera singer, Giacomo Rimini. She appeared with the tenor Volpi in "The Huguenots" at the Verona Opera, and is also remembered for her performances in "Norma" and "Turandot." During the 1930s, she served as a director at the Chicago Opera Company.

**Sabin, Albert Bruce (1906-1993):** Born to a traditional family of Bialystok Jews, Sabin invented the polio vaccine before dying in the United States. Sabin, who was considered by many to be the greatest pediatrician and physician-discoverer of the 20th century, received numerous honors, including 40 honorary doctorates and a nomination for the Nobel Prize.

**Sapirsztejn, Jakow (Anglicized to Jacob Sapirstein) (1884-1967):** Emigrated in 1905 to the United States, where he established a postcard company which grew to become the very successful American Greetings Corp. His son, **Irving I. Stone,** born in Cleveland in 1909, started at the company as a boy, and is now its Founder Chairman and Chairman of the Executive Committee.

**Shamir (Szamir), Yitzhak (1915- ):** This former prime minister of Israel (1983-84, 86-92) was born and raised in northeast Poland, near Bialystok. He attended his last two years of high school at the Hebrew Gymnasium in Bialystok.

**Simcha, Tzfas (1814-1917):** In 1842, the first Jew from Bialystok to arrive in America.

**Slonimski, Chaim Zelig (1810-1904):** Born in Bialystok, this gifted scientist and inventor is credited with inventing one of the earliest mechanical calculating machines. He won early acclaim for a text on astronomy, *The History of the Heavens (Toldot Haszmain)*, published in 1838. He also founded and published the Hebrew weekly, *Hacefira*, edited in Berlin and Warsaw. This was one of the first publications to stress the necessity of establishing a Jewish nation in Palestine.

**Solasz, Sam (1928- ):** Born in Knyszyn, near Bialystok, he escaped from a train enroute to Treblinka and survived the Holocaust. After the war he settled first in Israel and then moved to the United States in 1951. He founded what has become a large and successful meat company. He served for many years as President of the Bialystoker Center and Home for the Aged in New York City.

**Sukenik, Eliezer Lipa (1889-1953):** Born in Bialystok, he emigrated to Palestine in 1912. Studied at the Jerusalem Teachers

Seminary, at the Babylonic School of the Dominican friars, and at universities in Germany and the United States. He spent his career in the Archaeology Department of the Hebrew University, as a scholar from 1925 and then a professor from 1938. He earned an international reputation for his field work, including excavations (with Professor L.A. Meir) which exposed the "third wall" of Jerusalem, and his part in the discovery of the Dead Sea Scrolls, some of which he acquired for Jerusalem University. He researched Jewish synagogues and cemeteries from the Roam and Byzantine periods, and was a scholar of epigraphy and Hebrew numismastics. (Professor Sukenik's son, who was born in Jerusalem in 1917 and took the name **Yigal Yadin,** was an active member of the "Hagana" armed force before the state of Israel was founded, and later rose to prominence as a major general in the General Staff Command and Chief of Staff of the Israeli Defense Forces.)

**Weber, Max (1881-1961):** This celebrated painter, printmaker and sculptor, born in Bialystok, moved to New York City in 1891. After attending the Pratt Institute in Brooklyn from 1898 to 1900, he spent three years in Paris studying at the Académie Julian and with Henri Matisse. After a period of work influenced by the Fauvists, the Cubists, and the Futurists, he turned to more representational forms, marked by a personal expressionism and sense of humor. Many of the paintings of his later years dealt with Jewish, especially Hasidic, themes. Among his pupils at the Art Students League in New York was Mark Rothko.

**Wiener, Leo (1862-1939):** Philologist and writer. His birth certificate—in Russian and Hebrew—can be viewed in Bialystok's State Archives at 4 Rynek Kosciuszki.

**Zamenhof, Ludwik L. (1859-1917):** Born in a house on Zielona Street in Bialystok, Zamenhof invented and introduced Esperanto in 1887. Esperanto is an artificial "international" language designed to facilitate communication between speakers of different languages.

Bialystok: Advertisements in Esperanto, 1927 (collection TW)

# APPENDIX III

## Growth of Jewish Population in Bialystok (City)

| Year | Total Population | Number of Jews | Percent Jews |
|------|------------------|----------------|--------------|
| 1663 | 634 | 75 | 11.8% |
| 1765 | 3,400 | 761 | 22.4% |
| 1772 | 1,845 | 820 | 44.4% |
| 1788 | 3,930 | 1,768 | 45.5% |
| 1807 | 4,145 | 2,116 | 51.0% |
| 1808 | ca. 6,000 | ca. 4,000 | 66.6% |
| 1847 | unknown | 6,714 | |
| 1857 | 12,938 (13,787?) | 9,547 | 69 -73.8% |
| 1860 | 16,544 | 11,288 | 68.2% |
| 1861 | 17,000 | 11,873 | 69.8% |
| 1878 | 34,505 | 20,365 | 59.0% |
| 1895 | 62,993 | 47,783 | 76.0% |
| 1897 | 66,032 | 41,905 | 63.5% |
| 1910 | ca. 76,000 | 52,123 | 68.6% |
| 1913 | ca. 100,000 | 70,000 | 70.0% |
| 1914 | 89,703 | 61,500 | 68.6% |
| 1916 | 54,260 | ca. 40,000 | 73.7% |
| 1921 | 76,792 | 37,186 | 48.4% |
| 1931 | 91,355 | 39,165 | 42.9% |
| 1936 | 99,722 | 42,880 | 43.0% |
| 1939 (Oct.) | 200,000 | 140,000 | 70.0% |
| 1939 (Nov.) | 330,000-400,000? | 250,000? | 71.0% |
| 1941 (Oct.) | ca. 80,000 | ca. 50,000 | 62.5% |

# APPENDIX IV

## Bialystok Jewish Cemetery Names

The following names, with date of death, are among those on tombstones in the Bialystok cemetery which could be deciphered by the author in 1994:

1874 - Ester Rozental, daughter of Kaplan Zeew Wolf
1876 - Riwka, daughter of Manisza Warszawic
1880 - Rabin Dow Teper
1891 - Josef Markus
1892 - Jakow Szalom Godfarb, son of Icchok
1893 - Rachela Kaplan, daughter of Mosze Chackieles
1894 - Jehuda Wendel, son of Mordechaj
1894 - Kohen Eltanan, son of Jehudy Kaplan
1894 - Eltanan Kaplan, son Jehuda
1894 - Zusman Mejer Knyszynski, son of Szmuel Eli
1894 - Merka Lea Janower, daughter of Awigdor
1894 - Ari Lejb Kagan
1894 - Fruma Narewska, daughter of Mosze Cwi
1894 - Gitel, daughter of Lejb Biterman
1894 - Mosze Walach, son of Abrahama Jakow
1895 - Sara, wife of Jehoszua Rybalowski
1895 - Abraham, son of Jakow Barslowski
1895 - Malka, daughter of Mordechaj Gimpel
1896 - Todros Szturmak, daughter of Izrael
1896 - Eliezer Baruch, son of Josef from Trestiny (Trzcianne)
1896 - Sara Rabinowicz, daughter of Eliezer
1896 - Sima, daughter of Zelig Ahron Jaszinowski
1896 - Mosze Zelman Gerszon Nozyk
1897 - Dow Ber Dojlidzki, son of Mosze Szmuel
1897 - Jehudit Goldsztajn, daughter of Ari Lejb
1898 - Ginendel Mazur, daughter of Arie
1898 - Chaim Kalman Goldman
1898 - Jakow Dawid Borowski, son of Izrael
1898 - Szraga Fajwel Bloch, son of Jehoszua
1898 - Iszmar Beniamin Aronson
1898 - Rachel Leja Rozental
1898 - Zelda Lapidus, daughter of Lejb Jakow
1898 - Rajca Czarniecka, daughter of Eliezer Eli

1898 - Ida Borisowna Domaracka
1898 - Jehuda Mazur, son of Jakow
1898 - Chana Rubinstein
1899 - Malka Litwinska, daughter of Eli Cwi Litwinski z Charbina
1899 - Dawid Wilenski, son of Szmuel
1899 - Chana Ester Miedownik
1899 - Chana Basza Szczupak, daughter of Jehoszua
1899 - Israel Rafalowski, son of Jakow Lejb Halewi
1900 - Aron Minc Menachem Nachum
1900 - Chana Hendler
1900 - Kohen Cadok Pruzanski, son of Szmuel
1900 - Jekutiel Arie Sapirsztejn
1900 - Jakow Biber, son of Gerszon
1900 - Jakow Noach Szlachter, son of Mosze
1900 - Benjon Bloch, son of Alexander
1900 - Abraham Icchok Hendler
1901 - Icchok Lewinson, son of Mordchaj
1901 - Fruma Sztejn Chana, daughter of Natan
1901 - Murka Wigodska, daughter of Abraham Aszer Ginsburg
1901 - Mosze Chaim Winik, son of Szlomo Lejb
1901 - Maria Mina Kohn
1901 - Mordchaj Cwi Kostow (Kustow), son of Jehoszua
1901 - Fejgiel Tiferman, daughter of Jehoszuy Gaon
1902 - Cipora, daughter of Mosze Krinski
1902 - Rachela Wigdorowic, daughter of Gerszon Hefner
1902 - Ruth Judit Cytron
1902 - Mosze Lejb Miszondzik, son of Icchoka Eliezer
1902 - Chaim Wilenski, son of Josif Ari
1902 - Chana Zawadzka, daughter of Szlomo Miszondzik
1902 - Ari Lejb Ginsburg, son of Cwi Hakchen
1902 - Efraim Potocki, son of Natan
1902 - Liba, daughter of Mardche Lipkies
1903 - Beniamin Potocki, son of Nisan
1903 - Aron Makower, son of Josef Szlomo Mino
1903 - Joche Wilcik, daughter of Josif
1903 - Mosze Rotszild, son of Jehuda Hakohen
1903 - Icchok Rubinstejn, son of Abraham
1903 - Jakow Zelig, son of Jehoszua Kohen
1903 - Ester, daughter of Szlomo Lejb Grodzinski
1903 - Malka Rajzel Janowska, daughter of Mordche Lejb
1903 - Jakow Kac, son of Mosze Icchok Kohen Kac

1904 - Abraham icchok Radzinower, son of Josif
1904 - Arie Lejb Barasz
1904 - Masza Malka, daughter of Hanoch Pompianski from Wilna
1904 - Mejer Szlomo Sybirski, son of Nachum Mosze
1904 - Szlomo Zalman Hirszhorn, son of Zalman
1904 - Gedali Karowicki, son of Jehoszua
1905 - Miriam, daughter of Mosze Lipa Witraz
1905 - Chaim Lubliner, son of Beniamin Zeew Wolf
1905 - Chaim Lubliner, son of Cwi Hakohen
1905 - Ari Lejb Farber, son of Chaim
1905 - Mosze Kalmanowicz Falkowicz
1906 - Isachar Goldber, son of Jakow
1906 - Cwi Hirsz Smagler, son of Jehoszua
1906 - Ester Wasilkowska, daughter of Izrael Hakohen
1906 - Tojwe Heszel Kacenelbogen
1906 - Abraham Icchok Berinsztejn
1906 - Sara Dina, daughter of Szalom Cwi Jelin
1906 - Szlomo Falter Balter, son of Ario
1906 - Mosze Josif Rabinowicz
1906 - Dwora, daughter of Icchok Goldberg
1907 - Zlata Zibelman, son of Mosze Chaim Halewi
1907 - Handel Lubawski, daughter of Szalom Marion
1907 - Israel Litwak, son of Jakow Zeew
1907 - Ester Mindel Rubinsztejn
1907 - Chana Debora, daughter of Mordchaj Chaim Grinhauz
1908 - Fejga Majzler, daughter of Jakowa Iwanowskiego
1908 - Bejla Sopockowska, daughter of Josif
1908 - Calel Dawidowicz Szapiro
1908 - Eliezer Rabinowicz, son of Szloma
1908 - Zisel, daughter of Jakow Marano
1908 - Lipsza, daughter of Josef Eliezer Lewin
1909 - Icchok Briskier (Bryskier), son of Abraham
1909 - Cwi Ginsbur, son of Arie Lejb Hakohen
1909 - Rechama, daughter of Chaim Mosze Rabinowicz
1909 - Abraham Osipowicz Monachowski
1909 - Chaja Sara Koianska, daughter of Cwi Hirsz
1909 - Miriam Ester Goniodzka, daughter of Zeew
1909 - Dow Arie, son of Mosze Zalman Abersztejn
1909 - Szlomo Wajnsztajn
1909 - Icchok Gendelman, son of Dawid
1910 - Gitla Nejmark

1910 - Josef Dtewelowicz Swirski
1910 - Szmuel Aszer Dinowicz, son of Mordechaj
1910 - Jakow Szapiro
1910 - Daron Linczewski
1910 - Dawid Sidranski, son of Josef
1911 - Sara Liba Wajdenbaum
1911 - Sara Leja Barszczewska, daughter of Szymon
1911 - Estera, daughter of Samuel Tanchum Kadlubik
1911 - Lipa Witraz, son of Meir Cwi Hirsz
1911 - Pesach Czapnik, son of Nehemi Lewity
1911 - Sara, daughter of Nisen Potocka
1912 - Szifra Cyryl Tykocka, daughter of Josif Eliezer
1912 - Nachum Josif Sibirski
1912 - Jente Arie Lejb Szmerkes
1912 - Mordchaj Manes
1912 - Hesse Ozder, daughter of Cwi Zorach Kohen
1913 - Sara Chaja Gdanska, daughter of Mosze
1913 - Josef Fajbert, son of Josif Zelig Kohen
1913 - Chana Zabludowska, daughter of Abraham
1914 - Helka Sztejn, daughter of Gerszon
1916 - Jehoszua Arie Czaczkowski
1916 - Szabtaj Rozenblum, son of Icchok
1916 - Jechaskiel Rabinowicz, son of Chaima
1918 - Menachem Zak, son of Jehuda Lejb
1919 - Bluma Bacer
1920 - Miriam Rozental
1920 - Riwka Pat Mowszowicz, daughter of Chaima Mordchaj
1920 - Pasza Beja Gutmann, daughter of Cwi
1920 - Meir Sturmak, son of Todros
1921 - Jakow Szlomo Goldberg, son of Eli Chaim from Janow
1921 - Abraham Halper, son of Szlomo
1924 - Aron Lejb Szmidt, son of Jakow
1926 - Jehoszua Cwi Sarna
1927 - Lejba Zawadzka, daughter of Meir
1929 - Dina jogoda, daughter of Jonasz

Dates undecipherable:

Abraham Icchok Bielawski, son of Abraham Icchok
Mordchaj Zelig, son of Juda Cwi
Abraham Bunim, son of Josif Liberman

## Appendix V

## *Tykocin Jewish Cemetery Names*

The following names, with date of death, are among those on tombs in the Tykocin cemetery which could be deciphered by the author in 1994:

Mirel, daughter of Josif, 1791
Szfira, daughter of Abraham, 1815
Israel Jehuda, son of Jakow, 1885
Marejnu Menachem, son of Moshe Ben Eliezer, 1865
Rabin Moshe, son of Cwi, 1826
Bejle Dwora, daughter of Zeew Blumenfeld, 1830
Szinda, daughter of Moshe, 1826
Rebeka, daughter of Jakub, 1859
Jakow Cwi, son of Reb Ezra, 1866
Mirel, daughter of Heter, 1754
Szlomo Chaim, 1850
Mira Bejla, daughter of Harberman, 1836
Miriam, daughter of Josif Zysel, 1813
Hes, son of Pinchus, 1893
Sziloch, daughter of Josif, 1845
Cwi, 1813
Chaja, daughter of Jakow Mirel, 1881
Icchok, 1925
Menachem, 1885
Kreindel Miriam, daughter of Jehuda Segal, 1812
Miriam o Szlomo, 1866
Rachel, daughter of Mejer, 1876
Cwi Szlomo, son of Reb Benjamin Arie, 1900
Chawa, daughter of Abraham, 1892
Tanchum, son of Moshe Lewita, 1823

# Appendix VI

## Jewish Communities in the Bialystok Region Existing Before 1939

Some of the settlements included in the list below are not covered in the main text because nothing of the towns survives today.

| Settlement | The date of granting town privileges | First appearance of Jews | Establishment of the community |
|---|---|---|---|
| 1. Bialowieza | - | end 19th c. | 1910? |
| 2. Bialystok | 1691? | 1658 | 1691? |
| 3. Bielsk Podlaski | 1495 | 1487 | 1802 |
| 4. Bocki | 1509 | 1577 | 1578 |
| 5. Bransk | 1493 | 1613 | 1820 |
| 6. Choroszcz | 1507 | 1557 | 1566 |
| 7. Dabrowa Bial. | pre-1775 | beg. 18th c | 2d half 18th c. |
| 8. Drohiczyn | 1498 | 1487 | beg. 19th c. |
| 9. Grodek | beg. 16th c. | 1614 | end 17th c. |
| 10. Hajnowka | 1950 | end 19th c. | 1915? |
| 11. Jalowka | 1545 | 1690 | 1708 |
| 12. Janow Sokolski | 1791 | mid 17th c. | beg. 18th c. |
| 13. Jasionowka | 1642 | 16th c. | 17th/18th c. |
| 14. Kleszczele | 1523 | 1580 | 18th/19th c. |
| 15. Knyszyn | 1568 | 1605 | beg. 18th c. |
| 16. Korycin | 1671 | beg. 17th c. | beg. 18th c. |
| 17. Krynki | 1569 | beg. 17th c. | 1639 (1662?) |
| 18. Kuznica | 1546 | beg. 17th c. | pre-1623 |
| 19. Lapy | 1925 | mid 19th c. | 1880 |
| 20. Michalowo | - | beg. 19th c. | 1903 |
| 21. Mielnik | 1440 | 1533 | 1689 - 1694? |
| 22. Milejczyce | 1516 | 16th c. | mid 18th c. |
| 23. Narew | 1514 | 1560 | beg. 19th c. |
| 24. Narewka | pre-1794 | 18th/19th c | beg. 19th c. |
| 25. Niemirow | pre-1613 | 1708 | mid 18th c. |
| 26. Nowy Dwor | 1578 | 1540 | 1558 |
| 27. Orla | 1634 | 16th c. | 16th/17th c. |
| 28. Sidra | 1566 | end 17th c. | 17th/18th c. |
| 29. Siemiatycze | 1542 | 1582 | 1653 |

| | | | |
|---|---|---|---|
| 30. Starosielce | | | |
| (now district of Bialystok) | | 1772 | 1910 |
| 31. Sokolka | 1609˙ | mid 17th c. | 1698 |
| 32. Suchowola | pre-1777 | beg. 17th c. | 1698 |
| 33. Suprasl | after 1861 | beg. 17th c. | beg. 19th c. |
| 34. Suraz | 1445 | 1525 | beg. 19th c. |
| 35. Tykocin | 1425 | 1522 | 1522 |
| 36. Wasilkow | 1566 | 1653 | 1714 |
| 37. Zabludow | mid 16th c. | beg. 16th c. | 1566 |

Jews also lived in more than 100 different villages in the Bialystok region, usually running shops or inns. There were also Jewish villages created as a result of the Jewish settlement in the 19th century. Among the better known ones were Kolonia Izaaka (Issac's Colony) near Odelsk (today in Belarus), or the village Palestyna, which still exists today with the same name.

In the period between the two World Wars the movement towards farming among Jews gained popularity. Numerous rural colonies were organized by kibutz societes. Their task was to prepare Jews for farming in Palestine. The 1921 census revealed a number of Jewish communities in the small villages in the rural areas of the Bialystok region. In some villages there even were small prayer halls, as in Czarna Bialostocka, Pieniazki or Grodzisk. These symbolic synagogues were used for daily religious observations, while more important holidays were celebrated by going to synagogues in the larger towns.

## Villages where the census of 1921 noted more than 10 Jews living:

**Bialowieza district** (pre-war districts): Panasiuki - 17, Zastawa - 15, Krzyze - 10, Cichawola - 11, Masiewo - 26, Chwalowo - 24, Hlubieniec (colony) - 37, Izbice - 11, Krynica - 13, Pieniazki - 108, Popielewo - 12, Rowbick - 37, Suchowola - 46.

**Bialystok district:** Jakubiewo - 13, Mieleszki - 16, Kamienny Brod - 14, Laskowiec - 12, Zubole - 21.

**Bielsk Podlaski district:** Kalejczyce - 14, Krasna Wies - 12, Czarna Wies - 47, Grodzisk - 34, Makaraki - 17, Zery Czubiki - 11,

Hornowo - 16, Zurobice - 27, Czyzyki - 10, Dubiny - 20,
Grabowiec - 10, Kalnica - 10, Nurzec Stacja - 38, Rogacze - 23,
Sasiny Ostrow - 10, Sobiatyn - 15, Odrynki - 15, Buzyska - 11,
Chrolowice - 13, Obnizki - 13, Sieniewice - 33, Wierzchnica
Nadbuzna - 17, Holowieski - 19, Paszkowszczyznie - 16, Stary
Kornin - 10, Szczyty - 10, Czyze - 22, Borysowszczyzna - 16,
Radzilowka - 16, Czaje Wolka - 14, Rudka - 28, Annopol - 50,
Boratynie Lacki - 14, Glinnik - 12, Tolowin - 22, Granne - 14,
Pobikry - 12, Przybyszyn - 14, Falki Stare - 11, Malesze - 14,
Swirydy - 29, Polsze - 30, Holynka - 49, Kruszyniany - 21.

**Sokolka district:** Buksztel - 15, Wodokaczka - 23, Kruhly - 16,
Palestyna - 17, Jalowka Folwark - 12, Nietupa - 11,
Podsokolka - 12.

# Appendix VII

## Some Travel Basics for the Region

(*Note:* Although every effort has been made to update the information below, neither the author nor the publisher can assume responsibility for its accuracy. Prices are approximate. Readers are invited to submit corrections or recommendations to the author or the publisher. See note on back of title page.)

### Transportation

**Train** travel in Poland is inexpensive, on time, and generally comfortable. Most visitors find the first-class tickets worth the premium. Between Warsaw and Bialystok there is excellent service, and the trip takes a little less than three hours. One-way fare approximately $6.00-9.00. **Train station:** Kolejowa, tel. for information 910.

**Buses** are a good resource for travel between towns and villages in the rural areas. In Bialystok the intercity bus depot is one block from the train station. Round-trip fare to Warsaw is about $4.50-5.00. And within Bialystok itself there is an extensive and reliable bus system. Tickets are available at most of the ubiquitous kiosks. **Bus terminal:** Bohaterow Monte Cassino, tel. for information 936.

An **automobile** certainly would be preferred for any extended travel in the Bialystok region. Auto rentals are most easily arranged in the largest cities, Warsaw being the closest and offering the most choices; drivers also can be hired. For car rentals in Bialystok, try these numbers: 45.32.54 or 090 52.10.00; 61.56.50; 32.70.32, or after 5 p.m. 0 602 63.22.73; 75.49.26; 61.82.32, or 0 601 35.21.75.

**Taxis** are a good choice for travel around Bialystok; they are plentiful and inexpensive. Lines of waiting taxis can usually be found at several stands downtown. Several radio taxi companies also offer excellent service. To obtain one, dial one of these numbers: 32.32.32, 41.41.41, 44.44.44, 45.50.50, 919, or 96.21 through

28. You can also hire a taxi to travel from Bialystok to other towns; negotiate fares in advance.

## Money Exchange

Money should be changed only in the officially established *kantors* (exchange offices), or in the banks. The differences in exchange rates from one such place to another is minimal. The main thing is not to exchange money with unauthorized individuals.

## Telephoning

The country code for Poland is 48, the city code for Bialystok 85. So to call Bialystok direct from the U.S., dial 011-48.85, followed by the six-digit local number. Telephones and fax machines are readily available in hotels. Public phones are available elsewhere and require coins or a calling card.

## Accomodations

Choice of accomodations is rapidly improving throughout Poland. All the major cities now have good to excellent hotels. Many also offer bed and breakfasts, rooms in private homes, hostels, campgrounds and rental homes.

The following five Bialystok hotels all have rooms with private bath, TV, telephone and radio (except no radio at Pastel). They all have restaurants, bars and secure parking facilities, and accept major credit cards.

**Cristal,** Lipowa 3. Tel. 425-061, fax 425-800. Singles about $40.00, doubles $50.00, suites $80.00; breakfast included. Located in the center of the city, this hotel was renovated in 1993-94. Recommended.

**Pastel,** Waszyngtona 24A (about 1 km. from city center). Tel. and fax: 442-744, fax 423-387. Singles about $40.00, doubles $55.00-60.00, suites $80.00; breakfast included. This is a new hotel, opened in 1994. Recommended.

**Golebiewski,** Palacowa 7. Tel. 435-435, fax 537-399. Singles about $60.00, doubles $70.00-75.00; breakfast included. A large new hotel, near the city center, opened in 1996. Recommended.

**Lesny,** Zwyciestwa 77 (about 6 km. west of city center, on Highway 18). Tel. 511-641, fax 511-701, e-mail http://www.lesny-hot.optinet.pl. Singles about $35.00-40.00, doubles $50.00, suites $80.00; breakfast included.

**Turkus,** Zwyciestwa 54 (about 2 km. west of city center, on Highway 18). Tel. 513-278, fax 511-211. Singles about $30.00, doubles $40.00, suites $70.00-75.00; breakfast included.

*Restaurants*

Here are some recommended restaurants in the center of Bialystok:

**Astoria,** Sienkiewicza 4
**Pizzeria Avanti,** Sienkiewicza 24
**China Garden,** Pilsudskiego 23
**Cristal Hotel,** Lipowa 3/5
**Golebiewiski Hotel,** Palacowa 7
**Magnat,** Malmeda 3
**Premiera,** Piekna 2

*Museums*

These Bialystok museums are generally open from 10 a.m. to 5 p.m., Tuesday through Sunday, except on days following holidays:

**Regional Art Museum,** Rynek Kosciuszki 7 (in the Old City Hall building). Some fine late 19th- and early 20th-century Polish paintings.

**Sculpture Museum of Alfons Karny,** Swietojanska 17. Impressive sculptural art in an attractive setting.

**History Museum,** Warszawska 37. Has some interesting Jewish memorabilia, which may or may not be on display.

**Military Museum,** Kilinski 7. Uniforms and weapons through the ages provide an interesting perspective on Poland's history.

**Slendzinski Gallery,** Warynskiego 24a (at site of Cytron Synagogue). Collection of paintings by the talented Slendzinski family.

**Bialystok Village Museum,** on east side of Highway 19 (toward Augustow), about 5 km. north of downtown Bialystok.

### Bialystok Galleries

**Arkady Art Gallery,** Rynek Kosciuszki 15.
**Arsenal Art Gallery,** Mickiewicza (near Branicki Palace).
**Brama Art Gallery,** Kilinski 1.
**Friends of Art Association Gallery,** Warszawska 25.
**Cepelia,** Grochowa (near Lipowa). Polish handicrafts.
**Desa,** Rynek Kosciuszki. Antiques and art.

### Music

**Philharmonic Orchestra Hall,** Podlesna 3. Tel. 416-557. The Bialystok Symphony Orchestra generally has performances Thursday and Friday evenings in season. Closed during July and August.

### Other Important Basic Information

**Police,** tel. 997
**Fire,** tel. 998
**Emergency,** tel. 990, 999
**City Guard,** 520-083, 753-301

**Tourist information:**
• Tourist Information Office (including small Zamenhof Gallery), located in building of former synagogue at Piekna 1, tel. 441-742, tel. and fax 454-600; e-mail: citik@centrumtur.sitech.pl
• InfoBank about useful services, tel. 320-520 or 951
• Orbis Travel Agency, Rynek Kosciuszki

• Bird Service Tours, Popieluszki 105, 15-641 Bialystok, tel. and fax 616-768; specializing in nature tours, especially bird watching, which is exceptional in the Bialystok region.

**Main Post Office,** Warszawska 10, tel. 435-325; **other central offices** at Lipowa 32 and Rynek Kosciuski 32
**EMS-POCZTEX** (courier postal service), tel. 435-998
**United Parcel Service (UPS),** tel. 446-624
**DHL,** tel. (090)209-580

**City Hall,** Slonimska 1, tel. 322-089 or 329-325, fax 327-601, e-mail: city@cksr.ac.pl.bialystok. They have a useful WWW information page: http://falco.man.bialystok.pl/city
**Chamber of Commerce,** Spoldzielcza 8, tel. 411-404; tel. and fax 327-522
**City Archives,** Rynek Kosciuszki 4, tel. 435-506 or 435-655. Has birth, death and marriage certificates for Bialystoker Jews until 1896. Records from 1896 to date are at Branickiego 3.

*Travel Guidebooks*

An increasing number of travel guidebooks are available covering Poland. One that is particularly thorough and helpful is *Poland: The Rough Guide,* by Mark Salter and Gordon McLachland (New York: Viking Penguin, 1996). Another is *Poland: a Lonely Planet Travel Survival Kit,* by Krzysztof Dydynski (Hawthorn, Australia: Lonely Planet Publications, 1996).

A good book focussing especially on Jewish sites is Ruth Ellen Gruber's *Jewish Heritage Travel: A Guide to Central and Eastern Europe* (New York: John Wiley & Sons, Inc., 1992, 1994).

## Appendix VIII

## *Bibliography*

### I. General Reference and Reading

Barnavi, Eli, ed. *A Historical Atlas of the Jewish People.* New York: Schocken Books, 1995.

Folberg, Neil. *And I Shall Dwell Among Them: Historic Synagogues of the World* (with essay by Yom Tov Assis). New York: Aperture, 1995.

Frankel, Ellen. *The Encyclopedia of Jewish Symbols* (paper). Northvale, NJ: Jason Aronson, 1995.

Gruber, Ruth Ellen. *Jewish Heritage Travel: A Guide to Central and Eastern Europe.* New York: John Wiley & Sons, 1992, 1994.

——. *Upon the Doorsteps of Thy House: Jewish Life in East-Central Europe, Yesterday and Today.* New York: John Wiley & Sons, 1994.

Kanof, Abram. *Jewish Ceremonial Art.* New York: Harry N. Abrams, 1979

Krinsky, Carol Herselle. *The Synagogues of Europe: Architecture, History, Meaning.* Reprint of 1985 ed. New York andCambridge, MA: Dover Publications, 1996.

Loukomski, George. *Jewish Art in European Synagogues from the Middle Ages to the Eighteenth Century.* London: 1947.

Magocsi, Paul Robert. *Historical Atlas of East Central Europe.* Toronto: University of Toronto Press, 1996.

Meek, Harold A. *The Synagogue: The Complete History of the Art and Architecture of the Synagogue.* London: Phaidon/Chronicle Books, 1995.

Mendelsohn, Ezra. *The Jews of East Central Europe Between the Two Wars.* Bloomington: Indiana University Press, 1983

Myers, Phyllis. "The Old Shuls in Eastern Europe: Are They Worth Saving?" *Moment Magazine,* October 1990, p. 29.

Olitzky, Kerry M., and Ronald H. Isaacs. *A Glossary of Jewish Life.* Northvale, NJ: Jason Aronson, 1991.

Serotta, Edward. *Out of the Shadows: A Photographic Portrait of Jewish Life in Central Europe Since the Holocaust.* New York: Birch Lane Press, 1991.

Young, James. *The Texture of Memory: Holocaust Memorials and Meaning.* New Haven: Yale University Press, 1993.

## II. RELATED TO POLAND

Dobroszycki, Lucjan, and Barbara Kirshenblatt-Gimblett. *Image Before My Eyes: A Photographic History of Jewish Life in Poland Before the Holocaust.* New York: Schocken Books, 1977.

Gilbert, Martin. *Holocaust Journey: Travelling in Search of the Past.* New York: Columbia University Press, 1997.

Gruber, Samuel. "The Synagogues of Eastern Europe." *Metropolis Magazine,* June 1993.

Gruber, Samuel, and Phyllis Myers. *Survey of Historic Jewish Sites in Poland.* New York: World Monuments Fund, 1994.

Hoffman, Eva. *Shtetl: The Life and Death of a Small Town and the World of Polish Jews.* Boston: Houghton Mifflin, 1997.

Krajewska, Monika. *A Tribe of Stones: Jewish Cemeteries in Poland.* Warsaw: Polish Scientific Publishers, 1993.

Kugalmass, Jack, and Jonathan Boyarin, eds. *From a Ruined Garden: The Memorial Books of Polish Jewry.* New York: Schocken Books, 1985.

Piechotka, Maria and Kazimierz. *Wooden Synagogues.* Warsaw: 1959.

———. "Jewish Districts in the Spatial Structure of Polish Towns," in *Polin: A Journal of Polish-Jewish Studies,* vol. 5, pp. 24-39. Oxford: Basil Blackwell for the Institute of Polish-Jewish Studies, 1990.

———. *Bramy Nieba.* Warsaw: 1996.

Pisar, Samuel. *Of Blood and Hope.* Boston and Toronto: Little, Brown & Co., 1980.

Pogonowski, Iwo Cyprian. *Poland: A Historical Atlas.* New York: 1993.

Weiner, Miriam. *Jewish Roots in Poland: Pages from the Past and Archival Inventories.* New York: Miriam Weiner Routes to Roots Foundation/YIVO Institute for Jewish Research, in cooperation with the Polish State Archives, 1998. (To order, telephone 800-742-5403.)

### III. RELATED TO THE BIALYSTOK REGION

Archiwum Panstwowe w Bialymstoku (State Archives, Bialystok): records of births, marriages and deaths of the Jewish communities in the various towns of the region.

Archiwum Glowne Akt Dawnych w Warszawie (Main Archives of
Old Documents, Warsaw AGAD): Centralne Wladze
Wyznaniowe 1831 (Central Religious Authority, 1831); Akta
Komisji Rzadowej dotyczace gminy zydoskiej w Tykocinie,
1822-69 (Documents of the Government Commission relating
to the Jewish community in Tykocin, 1822-69).
Archiwum Panstwowe w Lomzy (State Archives, Lomza): Akta
dotyczace gminy zydowskiej w Tykocinie z XIX wieku do 1915
roku (Documents relating to the Jewish community in Tykocin
from the 19th century to 1915).
Gawurin, Alexsander. *Dzieje Zydow w Tykocinie, 1522-1795 (The
History of Jews in Tykocin, 1522-1795)*. Archiwum Zydowskiego
Instytutu Historycznego w Warszawie (Archives of the Jewish
Historical Institute in Warsaw), written before 1939.
Grajter, A., and Tomasz Wisniewski. Records of the Jewish ceme-
teries in Tykocin, Jasionowka, Narewka, Krynki, Suraz,
Choroszcz, Sokolka. Bialystok: State Agency for Protection of
Monuments in Bialystok (PSOZ, 23 Dojlidy Street). That agency
also has an interesting photo archive.
Herszberg, Abraham Samuel. *Pinkos Bialistok (Chronicle of
Bialystok)*. New York: Bialystok Jewish Historical Society, vol. I,
1949; vol. II, 1950.
Wisniewski, Tomasz. "The Linas Hatsedek Charitable Fraternity
in Bialystok, 1885-1939." In *Polin: A Journal of Polish-Jewish
Studies*, vol. 7, pp. 121-132. Oxford: Basil Blackwell for the
Institute of Polish-Jewish Studies, 1992.
———. *Synagogues and Jewish Communities in the Bialystok Region:
Jewish Life in Eastern Europe Before 1939*. Bialystok: David
Publishing House, 1992 (contains useful bibliography of 73
entries). *
*Yevreyskaya Enciklopedia*, vols. I-XVI. St. Petersburg: pre- World
War I.

* Copies of this hardcover book are available from Tomasz
Wisniewski at Box 351, 15-001 Bialystok. Fax: (48 85) 615.694. Web
site: http://www.gold-cousins.org/click on "Tomy Wisniewski."
Price U.S.$28.00, plus U.S.$12.00 for air mail shipment outside
Europe.  Inquire about prices for European delivery.

Mr. Wisniewski, the author of the present volume, also has an
extensive collection of photographs and postcards of Polish

Judaica, reproductions of which are offered for sale in attractive
sets at U.S.$12.00 plus U.S.$4.00 for air mail postage.

# Working Glossary of Terms Used in the Study of Jewish Art and Architecture

*Compiled by Samuel Gruber, Director of the Jewish Heritage Research Center, Syracuse, New York, and Adjunct Professor of Fine Arts at Syracuse University*

*Amidah*: Lit. "standing," from the position in which it is recited three times daily, this is the most essential part of the prayer service after the Shema. It is a series of benedictions expressing praise, thanksgiving, confession and petition.

*Ark*: Commonly used name for the *Aron-ha-Kodesh*.

*Ashkenazi*: Jewish cultural milieu, including Western, Central and Eastern Europe.

*Atarah*: Neckpiece for the *Tallit*, often of *Shpanyer Arbeit*.

*Avnet*: Torah binding.

*Besamim*: Spices for the *Havdalah* ceremony.

*Bet* (also *Beth*): Lit. "house," used as a prefix to denote specialized building types.

*Bet-Am*: Lit. "House of/for the People," an alternative name for the synagogue.

*Bet Din* (court): Rabbinic court.

*Bet ha-Chaim*: the house of garden of life, cemetery.

*Bet kewarot*: the house of place of graves (Neh. 2:3), cemetery.

*Bet-ha-Knesset* (BH): Lit., "House of gathering/assembly," synagogue.

*Bet-ha-Midrash*: Lit. "House of study." May also refer to a synagogue.

*Bet olam*: The house of eternity (Eccl. 12:5), cemetery.

*bimah* (*bema*): readers' platform in the synagogue.

*Binder* (Heb: *Avnet*): Belt that keeps the Torah scroll together while it is stored on the Ark. In some countries these were frequently made of circumcision cloths and embroidered with a name and date, to be used on the Bar Mitzvah.

breastplate: Common name for a *Tas*, the ornamental plate

hung on the front of a Torah scroll.

calligraphies: Ornate Hebrew writing, often creating designs
  incorporating scriptural or mystical text.
chai: Hebrew word for "life," often found on amulets.
chair of Elijah: Symbolic chair placed in vicinity of hechal.
challah: Painted loaves, two of which are blessed before
  Sabbath and festival meals.
Chevra Kaddisha: Lit. "Holy Society." Burial society, which
  looks after the needs attendant upon a death and funeral,
  beginning traditionally with the providing of watchers
  (Heb: shomrim) to be with the body from the moment of
  death until burial. The building located at the cemetery site
  used for the preparation of the body for burial is often
  referred to as the Chevra Kaddisha.
choshen: Torah breastplate, reminiscent of the breastplate
  worn by the Priest in the days of the Temple.
chuppah: Wedding canopy.
crown: Common name for a Keter.
Curtain for the Torah Ark (parochet): A curtain hung in front
  of the Torah Ark in synagogues.

dayyan: Leader of service.
Decalogue (Tablets of the Law): Stone tablets given by God to
  Moses on Mount Sinai, on which were inscribed the Ten
  Commandments. In recent centuries, an artistic represen-
  tation was frequently featured in the synagogue.

Eternal Light: A continuously burning lamp that hangs before
  the Torah Ark in a synagogue.
ethrog: A citrus fruit, used together with a lulav on Sukkoth.
Etz Hayim (pl. Azei Hayim): Hebrew for "Tree of Life." The
  roller for a Torah scroll.
esnoga: Sephardi term for synagogue.

Finial: Decorative terminal, mounted at the end of an Etz
  Hayim; correctly called a Rimmon.

geniza (genizah): Place for storing worn-out scrolls and
  religious books.

*haggadah*: Liturgy read at the *Seder*, and the book that
   contains it.
*halakha* (*Halaka*): The laws, rules and regulations which
   govern every phase of Jewish life and human relations,
   not only religious, but also domestic, social and political.
*hakafot*: The processional throughout the synagogue, led by
   one holding the torah scroll, generally prior to reading the
   Torah. It takes on special significance on *Simchat Torah*.
*Ha'Melech*: Rare type of Esther scroll in which each column,
   except the first begins, with the word *Ha'Melech*, "the
   King."
*Hanukah* (also *chanukah*): Mid-winter festival of lights.
*Hanukiyah*: Candelabrum used at Hanukah, also called a
   *Menorah*.
*Hasid* (pl. *Hasidim*; also *Chassid*): Member of mystic sect
   founded in Poland in 18th century, emphasizing joyful
   worship of an immanent God.
*Havdalah*: Ceremony concluding the Sabbath on Saturday
   evening
*Hazzan*: Cantor.
*hechal* (*ark*): Cabinet in which Torah scrolls are kept in a
   synagogue. Originally freestanding against the eastern wall
   of the synagogue, often placed in a niche or apse. Generally
   approached by steps and covered with an embroidered
   curtain.
*Hevrah Kadishah*: Burial society in a Jewish community.
*hillaulah*: Annual pilgrimage to tomb of revered rabbi or
   other holy personage.

Islamic Arches: Arches derived from Islamic architecture,
   usually horseshoe in profile and slightly pointed at the top.

*Judenstern*: Star-form, oil-burning hanging lamp for the
   Sabbath.

*Kaddish*: a hymn in praise of God, recited as part of the daily
   service or, in one form, as a mourner's prayer.
*kahal*: Jewish community.
*kamea*: Talisman or amulet.
*kappel*: Yiddish name for a skullcap.
*kasher*: "Fit for use"; applied to food and to objects, such as

Torah scrolls, which must be complete and undamaged
(Ashkenazi form "*Kosher*").

*keter*: Crown, usually to fit over the Torah when not in use.
*Ketubah*: Marriage contract.
*kiddush*: Prayer recited over wine on Sabbaths and festivals.
*kippa*: Modern Hebrew name for a skullcap.

*Ladino*: A Sephardi language, blending Hebrew and
medieval Spanish.
*Lulav*: A palm leaf with sprigs of myrtle and willow, used
with an *Ethrog* on Sukkoth.

*Ma'ariv*, or Arvit: Evening service.
*Magen David*: Star of David.
*Mahzor*: Prayer book containing the prayers according to the
cycle of the year.
*Mappah* (Torah Cover): A textile used to cover the Torah
between readings.
*matsah*: Unleavened bread eaten at Passover to commemorate
the Exodus.
*matzevah* (pl. *matzevot*), or *mazeva*. Gravestone.
*mechitzah*: Divider separating men's and women's sections
of synagogue.
*Megillah*: Manuscript Book of Esther recited on Purim.
*Me'il*: Protective mantle for the Torah scroll.
*mellah*: Jewish quarter in Moroccan town.
memorial lamp: Oil lamps, often in bronze, hung in a
synagogue and lit in memory of deceased congregant
on the anniversary of his or her death.
*menorah* (pl. *menorot*): A seven-branched candelabrum
found in the biblical sanctuary and Jerusalem Temple;
a similar candelabrum found in a synagogue; an eight-
branched candelabrum used during the Hanukah festival.
*mezuzah*: Small scroll fixed to the right doorpost as one
enters each door.
*mihrab*: Islamic arch motif, found on much Near Eastern
Judaica.
*mikvah* (pl. *mikvot*): (Ritual bath.) Facility employing fresh-
flowing water, used for monthly cleansing ritual for
women, and used for analogous rituals by men. Generally
not used by Jews who follow Reform tendencies. Ritual

baths were usually located near or even below the
synagogue or community center.

*Minchah* service: Afternoon service at synagogue.

*Minhagim*: Jewish customs.

*minyan*: Ten adults required for the reciting of prayers limited
to community recitation.

*Mishnah*: Digest of oral Torah teachings compiled about
200 CE.

*Mizrah* panel: Mizrah means east, the direction faced during
prayer; the name of decorative panels indicating direction.

*mohel*: Performer of ritual circumcision.

*muqarnas*: Derived from Islamic architecture.

*Ner Tamid*: The eternal light in the synagogue, in front of the
*Aron-ha-Kodesh*, meant to remind of the omnipresence of
God.

*ohel*: Lit. "tent," referring to a small structure built over a
tomb, usually of a rabbi or holy man.

*parochet*: Curtain in front of Ark in a synagogue.

*passul*: Invalid for ritual use; the opposite of *kasher*.

*Pentateuch*: Greek word for Five Books of Moses.

*Pesach*: Passover holiday.

pointer: Common name for a *Yad*, which is hung from the
*Etz Hayim* when not in use.

*Purim*: Festival commemorating the events in the Book of
Esther.

Reader's Desk: Table on which the Torah is placed for
reading; in Hebrew, *tevah* or *bemah*.

Reader's Desk Cover: A textile placed on the reader's desk.

*Rimmon(im)* (Finials): In Hebrew, lit. "pomegranate(s)";
adornment for the staves of the Torah scroll.

*Rosh Hashanah*: The Jewish New Year.

*Seder:* Ritual meal held at home on Passover eve.

*Seder* (or *siddur*) *tefillah*: Prayer book which includes
regular prayers for the whole year.

*Sephardi*: Referring to Jewish traditions originating in Spain
and spreading throughout the world after the expulsion of

the Jews from Spain in 1492.

*Sepher Torah* (pl. *Sifrei*):  Hebrew for "Torah scroll."

*Shabat*:  The Sabbath, which begins at sundown on Friday and continues until nightfall on Saturday (Ashkenazi pronunciation "Shabbos").

*Shaharit*:  Morning service.

*Shammash*:  In Hebrew, lit. "servant" or "one who ministers"; used to designate a synagogue functionary (sexton) and the candle or light on the Hanukah lamp that kindles (serves) the eight other lamps.

*Shavuoth*:  Pentecost, the first-fruits festival, marking the giving of the Law.

*Shivah*:  Seven days when it is a duty to visit the bereaved and comfort them.  In the house of mourning prayers are said on seven consecutive days.  The mourners refrain from attending any social events and celebrations, and from working or studying religious texts.  They just pray, sitting on the floor or on low stools as a sign of grief (the origin of the phrase "to sit *shivah*").  After the funeral of close relatives the mourning period is 30 days—the month of mourning. After the death of a parent the mourning lasts for 11 months—the year of mourning.

*Shofar*:  Ram's horn, sounded in synagogue on the New Year.

*Shpanyer Arbeit* (Yiddish for "Spanish work"):  Textiles of silver- or gold-wrapped thread.

*Shtetl*:  A former Jewish town or village in Eastern Europe.

*Sifrei Torah*:  Torah scrolls.

study house:  School and religious discussion room for Jewish male adults.  It is holier than a synagogue in religious standing.  It may be annexed to a synagogue or separately built, either in a purpose-built structure or in a room in a building used for other activities.  It may have an *ark* and a *bimah* so that people can use it for prayer.  It may be called in Yiddish a *kloyz* or *shtihl* (cf. German Klaus, Stube), especially if it is private (rather than owned by a congregation or by an officially designated Jewish community), or if it is used by Hasids.

*Sukkah*:  Leafy hut or "tabernacle" used on Sukkoth.

*Sukkoth*:  Seven-day Feast of Booths, originally a harvest festival.  The celebration takes place at home, in a booth decorated with branches, fruits and flowers.  A booth of this

sort may be erected also in a synagogue courtyard or on a
synagogue terrace.

*Tallit*:  Four-cornered prayer shawl worn by males for
morning prayers.

*Talmud*:  Record of legal decisions and discussions of ancient
Jewish sages, the fundamental work of the Oral Law that
complements the Written Law (*Pentateuch*).  There are two
versions of the Talmud: "Babylonia," and "Palestinian" or
"Jerusalem."  Each is divided into the *Mishnah* and the
*Gemara*.

*tas*:  Torah shield or breastplate.

*teffilin*:  "Phylacteries"; two small leather cases containing
parchment texts, worn by males at weekday morning
prayers.

*tevah (bimah)*:  Platform or table in a synagogue from which
the Torah scroll is read.  The platform supporting a
table is often of squarish or polygonal shape, and usually
is approached by steps on two sides.  A railing for security
and beauty encloses it.  The *bimah* is usually placed on the
main (east-west) axis, in the center in Ashkenazic Orthodox
synagogues, at the east end in Ashkenazic Reform synagogues, and opposite the ark in Sephardic-, Italian- and
Comtadin-rite synagogues.

*tiq (tik)*:  Near Eastern wood or metal case for the Torah scroll.

*Torah*:  Written Law, the Pentateuch.  Handwritten on parchment scrolls, it is kept in the synagogue ark.

Torah Crown (*Keter Torah*):  Adornment for the staves of a
Torah scroll.

*tsedakah*:  Charity.

*tsitsit*:  Ritual fringe on each corner of the *Tallit*.

wainscoting:  Continuous covering of lower walls, usually of
wood or tile.  In Moroccan synagogues tile wainscoting
sometimes extended as high as windows, and wooden wainscoting was attached to benches that lined the walls.

*wimpel*:  Fabric binder for when the Torah scroll is not in use.

*yad*:  Torah pointer.

*yarmulka*:  Russian or Polish name for the skullcap.

*Yahrzeit*:  The anniversary according to the Jewish calendar of

the death of a parent or other member of the immediate
family, commemorated by the lighting of a 24-hour candle
(yahrzeit candle), the saying of *Kaddish*, etc.
Yiddish:  An Ashkenazi language, blending Hebrew with
medieval German; written in the Hebrew alphabet, it contains vocabulary borrowings from Russian, Polish, English.
*Yom Kippur*:  Day of Atonement.

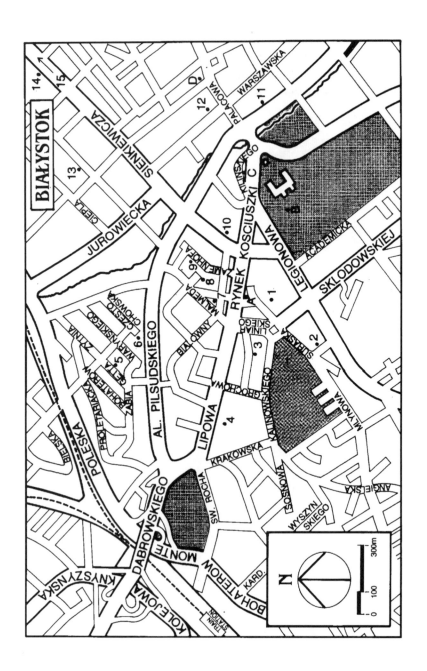

# APPENDIX X

## Key to Bialystok Map Locations

### Jewish Historical Sites

1. Site of the Great Synagogue
2. Site of Piaskower Synagogue
3. Site of Jewish Community Center and Library of Religious Books
4. Former Jewish Artisans' School
5. Ghetto Cemetery and Memorial Park
6. Site of Cytron Synagogue
7. Zamenhof statue

8. Malmeda plaque
9. Zamenhof birthplace
10. Former Jewish home, now Theater School
11. Site of Shmuel Synagogue
12. Former Jewish Maternity Hospital
13. Former Jewish Hospital
14. Former Hebrew Gymnasium
15. To Jewish Cemetery and Forest memorial

### Other Landmarks

A. Site of Old Town Hall
B. Branicki Palace and Gardens
C. Site of Ritz Hotel
D. Present Town Hall

TOMASZ WISNIEWSKI, born in 1958, is the author of three earlier books: *Ludwik Zamenhof, Bialystok in Old Postcards* and *Synagogues and Jewish Communities in the Bialystok Region.* A journalist and dedicated historian, Wisniewski is an acknowledged expert on Jewish landmarks and Jewish history in the Bialystok region of Poland. A non-Jew, he became interested in, and studied, the region's Jewish heritage while

jailed in Poland for dissident activities during the Communist period of martial law in the 1980s.

Wisniewski is a graduate of Warsaw University. He has also studied in Russia, Belarus, Lithuania, Israel (Beth Hatefutsoth, Yad Vashem) and in the United States (YIVO Institute). Now a newspaper editor in Bialystok, he also manages a genealogical service specializing in research in Bialystok, Suwalki, Lomza, Grodno and Brest. He and his wife live in Bialystok. His address is Box 351, 15-001 Bialystok, Poland; fax (48 85) 634 694. E-mail: tomekwisniewski@vena.telbank.pl *or* twisniewski@kurier-poranny.com

Readers can learn more about Wisniewski and his work by visiting these World Wide Web links:
http://www.gold-cousins.org/ Click on "Tomy Wisniewski"
http://www.megsinet.com/mikerose/ Click on "Synagogues"
http://www.geocities.com/Paris/Rue/4017/
　　Click on POLISH FRIENDS —> TOMEK WISNIEWSKI
http://www.scruz.net/~elias/hnoh
　　Click on JEWISH GENEALOGY and next
　　JUDAICA, JUDAICA, JUDAICA

---

MIMI SHERATON has been a food critic and travel writer for forty years, most notably at *The New York Times, TIME,* and *The Condé Nast Traveler.* She is the author of thirteen books, the latest of which is *Food Markets of the World* (Abrams). Her next book will be *The Oral History of the Bialy.*

*Notes*

*Notes*

*Notes*

*Notes*

*Notes*

*Notes*

*Notes*

*Notes*